# Tips for G
# Document D

- Try not to use too many fonts or text effects. Often good results can be gained from restricting yourself to two basic fonts: one for headings and one for body text.

- Allow yourself the use of white space. It is usually not necessary to completely fill the page, and space can be used as a very effective way of adding emphasis.

- Make sure that your text is always readable. More than 40 characters (or 10 words) to a line puts a strain on the human eye. Also, too little space between lines can create a solid mass of text which is very tiring to read.

- Use styles as much as possible. This way you have the flexibility to make design alterations to, for example, all your headings in one simple manoeuvre at any time.

- Make sure your document has a clear structure. In particular, check that main headings are obviously more prominent than sub-headings.

- Check the available templates to see if there is a ready-made document which suits your purposes. If not, you may still be able to adapt an existing template in order to create your own.

- Feel free to experiment with dummy text and graphics in the early stages of your design. Try to form a clear idea of which settings to use for document margins, text columns and page structure right from the beginning of your work.

- Consider creating 'roughs'. These are quick sketches which indicate roughly where the text and any graphics will appear on the page. This will help you see the overall effect of your ideas on paper, and will help you to decide on your final design.

- Keep your design as simple and consistent as possible.

_Handy Reference_

## Moving

| | |
|---|---|
| **Cursor keys** | Up/down/left/ right one space |
| **Ctrl+left/right** | Previous/next word |
| **Ctrl+up/down** | Previous/next paragraph |
| **Home/End** | Beginning/end of line |
| **Ctrl+Home/End** | Beginning/end of document |
| **PgUp/PgDn** | Move up/down one screen |
| **Ctrl+PgUp/PgDn** | Move to top/ bottom of window |
| **Alt+Shift+Up/Down** | Select paragraph and move up/down |

## Editing

| | |
|---|---|
| **Ctrl+NumPad5** | Select entire document |
| **Alt+Shift+NumPad5** (Numlock off) | Apply normal style |
| **Return** | New paragraph |
| **Shift+Return** | New line within paragraph |
| **Ctrl+Return** | New page |
| **Ctrl+Shift+Return** | New column |
| **Ctrl+Shift+*** | Display paragraph symbols |
| **Ctrl+Backspace** | Delete word to left |
| **Ctrl+Delete** | Delete word to right |
| **Ctrl+Shift+C** | Copy format |
| **Ctrl+Shift+V** | Paste format |

## Quick Formatting

| | |
|---|---|
| **Ctrl+B** | Bold |
| **Ctrl+I** | Italic |
| **Ctrl+Shift+A** | All caps |
| **Ctrl+Shift+K** | Small caps |
| **Ctrl+U** | Normal underline |
| **Ctrl+Shift+D** | Double underline |
| **Ctrl+Shift+W** | Word underline |
| **Ctrl+Shift+P** | Enter point size |
| **Ctrl+Shift+F** | Enter font |
| **Ctrl+=** | Subscript |
| **Ctrl++** | Superscript |
| **Ctrl+Shift+>** | Increase size |
| **Ctrl+Shift+<** | Decrease size |
| **Ctrl+]** | Increase by 1 point |
| **Ctrl+[** | Decrease by 1 point |
| **Ctrl+Space** | Reset format to current style |
| **Ctrl+Shift+S** | Select style |
| **Ctrl+L** | Left align |
| **Ctrl+E** | Centre align |
| **Ctrl+R** | Right align |
| **Ctrl+J** | Justify |
| **Ctrl+M** | Indent |
| **Ctrl+Shift+M** | Decrease indent |
| **Ctrl+T** | Hanging indent |
| **Ctrl+Shift+T** | Decrease hanging indent |
| **Ctrl+1** | Single line spacing |
| **Ctrl+2** | Double line spacing |
| **Ctrl+5** | 1.5 line spacing |
| **Ctrl+Shift+Q** | Apply Symbol font |
| **Ctrl+K** | Insert hyperlink |

## Menu Options

| | |
|---|---|
| **Ctrl+N** | New |
| **Ctrl+O** | Open |
| **Ctrl+W** | Close |
| **Ctrl+S** | Save |
| **Ctrl+P** | Print |

*Handy Reference*

| | |
|---|---|
| **Ctrl+Z** | Undo |
| **Ctrl+Y** | Redo |
| **Ctrl+X** | Cut |
| **Ctrl+C** | Copy |
| **Ctrl+V** | Paste |
| **Ctrl+A** | Select All |
| **Ctrl+F** | Find |
| **Ctrl+H** | Replace |
| **Ctrl+G** | Go To |
| **Alt+Ctrl+N** | Normal view |
| **Alt+Ctrl+P** | Page Layout |
| **Ctrl+D** | Font dialog |
| **Alt+Ctrl+K** | AutoFormat |

## Function Keys

| | |
|---|---|
| **F1** | Help |
| **Shift+F1** | Context-sensitive help |
| **F2** | Move selected text |
| **Shift+F2** | Copy selected text |
| **Ctrl+F2** | Print preview |
| **Shift+F3** | Change case |
| **Ctrl+F3** | Cut to Spike |
| **Ctrl+Shift+F3** | Insert spike |
| **F4** | Repeat previous command |
| **Shift+F4** | Find/Go To again |
| **Ctrl+F4** | Close document window |
| **Alt+F4** | Exit |
| **F5** | Go To |
| **Shift+F5** | Go back |
| **Ctrl+F5** | Restore document window |
| **Ctrl+Shift+F5** | Bookmark |
| **Alt+F5** | Restore Word window |
| **F6** | Next pane |
| **Shift+F6** | Previous pane |
| **Ctrl+F6** | Next document window |
| **Ctrl+Shift+F6** | Previous document window |

| | |
|---|---|
| **F7** | Spelling and Grammar |
| **Shift+F7** | Thesaurus |
| **Ctrl+F7** | Move document window |
| **Ctrl+Shift+F7** | Update links |
| **F8** | Extend selection |
| **Shift+F8** | Reduce selection |
| **Ctrl+F8** | Resize document window |
| **Ctrl+Shift+F8** | Select column |
| **F9** | Update field |
| **Shift+F9** | Display selected field on/off |
| **Ctrl+F9** | Insert field manually |
| **Ctrl+Shift+F9** | Unlink field |
| **Alt+F9** | Display all fields on/off |
| **Alt+Shift+F9** | Activate field |
| **F10** | Activate menu |
| **F11** | Next field |
| **Shift+F11** | Previous field |
| **Ctrl+F11** | Lock field |
| **Ctrl+Shift+F11** | Unlock field |
| **F12** | Save As |
| **Shift+F12** | Save |
| **Ctrl+F12** | Open |
| **Ctrl+Shift+F12** | Print |

## Special Characters

| | |
|---|---|
| **Ctrl+Shift+Space** | Non-breaking space |
| **Ctrl+Hyphen** | Optional hyphen |
| **Ctrl+Shift+Hyphen** | Non-breaking hyphen |
| **Ctrl+Tab** | Insert Tab (into table) |
| **Alt+0xxx** (on numeric keypad) | Insert ANSI character code 0xxx |

# WORD 97

## in easy steps

SCOTT BASHAM

COMPUTER STEP

**In easy steps** is an imprint of Computer Step
Southfield Road . Southam
Warwickshire CV47 OFB . England

http://www.ineasysteps.com

## Notice of Liability

Every effort has been made to ensure that this book contains accurate
and current information. However, Computer Step and the author shall
not be liable for any loss or damage suffered by readers as a result of
any information contained herein.

## Trademarks

Microsoft® and Windows® are registered trademarks of Microsoft
Corporation. All other trademarks are acknowledged as belonging to
their respective companies.

Printed and bound in the United Kingdom

ISBN 1-874029-68-7

# Table Of Contents

## 9 Templates and Wizards                              97

## 10 Graphical Features                                107

# Tables and Charts 123

## 11

# On-line and Internet Documents 139

## 12

# Index 153

# Getting to Know Word

This chapter gets you started with Word 97 quickly. It explains the screen layout, and introduces the various viewing modes that you can use to display your documents. Finally, it covers Word's extensive Help facilities.

## Covers

Chapter One

# Introduction

Word-processing was one of the first popular applications for the modern personal computer. In the early days it provided little more than the ability to enter and change text on a computer monitor. As time went on software and hardware improved, and features such as spell-checking and various type effects were added. Also, the number of users increased.

Microsoft Word 97 for Windows is widely acknowledged as a leader in its field, and is one of the best selling packages in any software category.

Let's face it, with Word 97 we're talking about a *big* package. It has retained the position as market leader by stuffing itself full of useful features, taking it from word-processing into the realms of graphical and data-oriented documents, and adding the capacity for Internet communications. At first it may seem to contain a bewildering array of options and controls, but many are there to make life easier – providing quick access to the most commonly used features.

A big package inevitably comes with a depressingly big reference manual, which will describe each and every function in minute detail. This book is not intended to replace the manual; instead you should view it as a more graphical teaching guide. Wherever possible, pictures and examples are used rather than pages of text to explain and demonstrate the concepts covered.

To gain maximum benefit from this book:

- Make sure that you are first familiar with the Windows operating environment (i.e. using a mouse, icons, menus, dialog boxes etc.).

- It is important to experiment using your own examples; like many things you will find that practice is the key to competence.

# The Word 97 Screen

Start Word by selecting Programs > Microsoft Word from the Start menu. You should see the following screen.

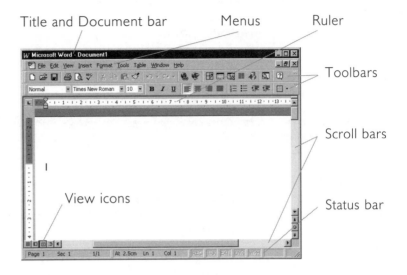

Title and Document bar    Menus    Ruler

Toolbars

Scroll bars

View icons

Status bar

Don't worry if the screen you see has extra items or things missing; you'll see in a moment that it's possible to configure the Word 97 screen in different ways.

*To quickly activate a toolbar, right-click the mouse on any currently visible toolbar to display a shortcut menu (see opposite). Check the toolbar of your choice.*

*To deactivate a toolbar, follow the same procedure, but instead uncheck the toolbar in the shortcut menu.*

## Toolbars

Toolbars can appear at the top of the screen, at the bottom, or as floating palettes. They give you instant access to features without the need to search through menus and dialog boxes. There are thirteen toolbars in total, but we usually only require several at any time.

## Activating/Deactivating Toolbars

1  Go to the View menu and choose Toolbars

2  Make sure that all are switched off except for "Standard" and "Formatting".

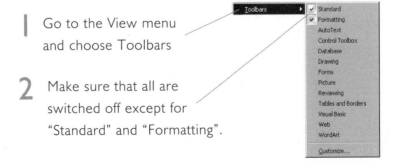

# Page Views

There are five different ways of viewing the page, which you can select from the top section of the View menu: *Normal*, *Online Layout*, *Page Layout*, *Outline* and *Master Document*.

## Normal View

This view allows fast editing, previewing most text effects, but does not display images and other objects.

*The first four of these views can be selected from the view icons at the bottom left of the Word 97 screen; all of them (including Master Document view) can be selected from the View menu.*

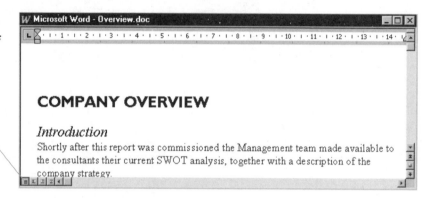

## Online Layout View

This makes online reading easier by displaying text larger than it will print at, and by displaying the Document Map, a tool you can use to move easily through your document.

*In any of these views, paragraph symbols (markers denoting carriage returns, spaces, etc) are by default not visible. To display them, click on the Paragraph Symbols icon in the Standard toolbar:*

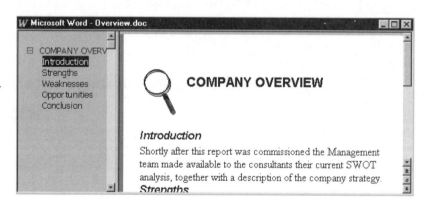

### Page Layout View

This view displays your document as actual pages, previewing text and graphics effects.

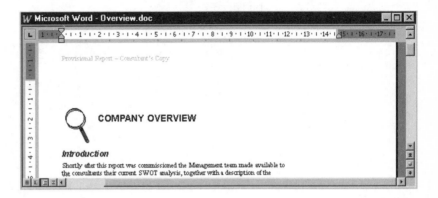

### Outline View

This allows you to view your text as a structured outline. Each major heading is marked with a plus-sign; subordinate headings are marked with a minus sign. To collapse a heading so that subordinate headings are not displayed, double-click on the plus-sign.

*The structure of a document can be rearranged from Outline view by dragging the plus- and minus-signs to another part of the document.*

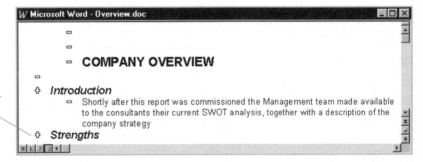

### Master Document View

This uses the same basic display as Outline view, but is used for long or structured documents. It allows you to alter the format of several related documents by changing a single master document which governs them.

# Adjusting the Page Setup

Go to the File menu and choose "Page Setup". The Page Setup dialog box appears. Like many of Word's dialog boxes, it is *tabbed*, i.e. subdivided into sections. You can select your required section by clicking on the appropriate tab at the top of the box.

1 Make sure the Margins tab is selected

2 Type in any required changes to the margin or header/footer dimensions

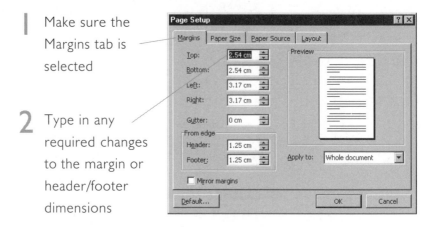

3 Click on the Paper Size tab

*You can also select tabs by pressing the Alt key together with the underlined letter in the tab name.*
*Alternatively, pressing Control together with the Tab key itself will cycle through each tab in turn.*

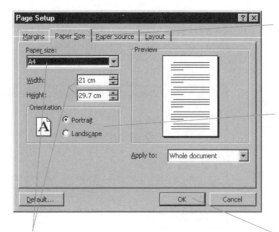

5 Select a page orientation: Portrait (tall) or Landscape (wide)

4 Select a paper size from the drop-down list, or enter custom values in the Width and Height boxes

7 Click OK to apply your changes

6 Make any necessary changes in the Paper Source and Layout tabs

# Help

Word 97 features several basic ways of offering you help. In increasing order of sophistication, these are Help boxes, on-line Help files, and (for users of Microsoft Office) the Assistant.

## Help Boxes

If you allow your mouse pointer to rest over an icon for a moment, a Help box will appear. This gives you a brief explanation of the icon's function.

Help box

## On-line Help Files

To access the on-line Help files, select Contents and Index from the Help menu. You then have three options. From the Contents tab, you can select the information you need by double-clicking on the structured Help category icon ● until you come to the specific topic ? you need; from the Index tab, you can select the Help topic you want from a simple list; or from the Find tab you can automatically search through all of the Help database for instances of a specific word or phrase.

## The Assistant

This is a very cute way of offering you help on whatever task you are performing. If the Assistant (an animated character with its own window) isn't already displayed, select "Microsoft Word Help" from the Help menu.

1 To get help, click anywhere within the Assistant window.

2 Enter some text relating to the information you want, then click Search...

3 Or click Tips for context-sensitive suggestions.

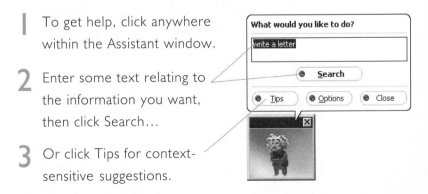

If the Assistant has a suggestion about the task you are currently performing, a light-bulb will appear in the window:

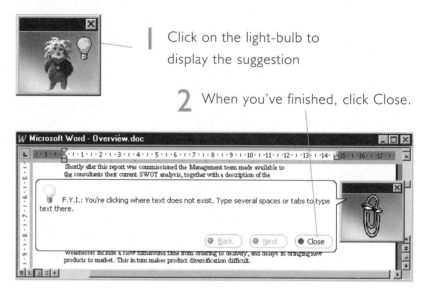

| Click on the light-bulb to display the suggestion

2 When you've finished, click Close.

## Changing the Assistant

If you get tired of your assistant, you can choose another. Insert your Office CD, then do the following:

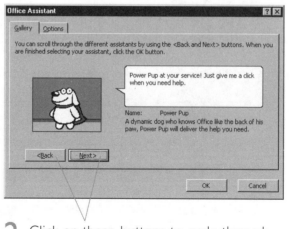

| Right-click anywhere in the Assistant's window and select "Choose Assistant" from the menu.

2 Click on these buttons to cycle through the different Assistants, then click OK.

# Basic Text Manipulation

This chapter helps you start entering and manipulating text on the screen. It looks at different ways of editing and formatting type, as well as saving and printing your work.

## Covers

**Chapter Two**

# The Document Window

The New
Document icon

1 If there is no Document window, then create a new one by clicking on the "New" icon in the top left of the standard toolbar.

2 Enter a sentence of example text.

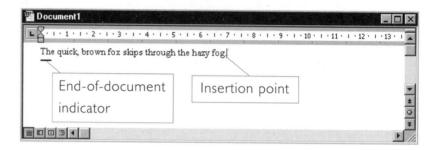

The vertical line is your *insertion point*, indicating where new text will appear. You can move the insertion point by:

*   Using the cursor (arrow) keys.

*   Clicking a new position with the mouse.

*Word auto-matically works out when to take a new line without breaking words. If you want to start a new paragraph, press the Return or Enter key.*

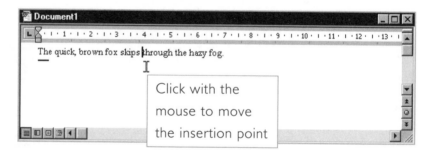

## Inserting Text

1 Move the insertion point to a point where you would like to add more text.

2 Type the text. It will appear at the insertion point.

Note that the words to the right of the insertion point move along to accommodate the new text:

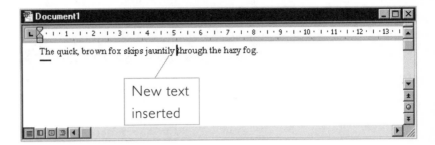

New text inserted

## Deleting Text Using Backspace

Move the insertion point so that it is directly after the text you want to delete.

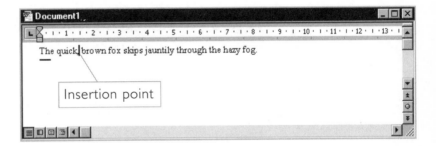

Insertion point

2 Press the Backspace key once to erase each character to the *left* of the insertion point.

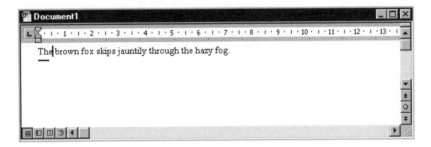

## Deleting Text with the Delete Key

1 This time move the insertion point before the text to be deleted.

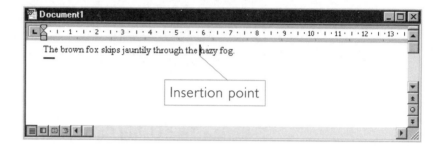

2 Press the Delete key once to erase each character to the *right* of the insertion point.

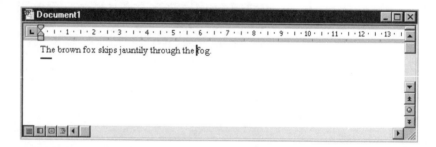

## Selecting Text

You can select text by using the mouse to drag horizontally across it, while holding down the left button:

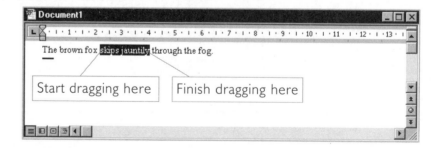

### Replacing Selected Text

Anything you type will automatically replace any text which is currently selected:

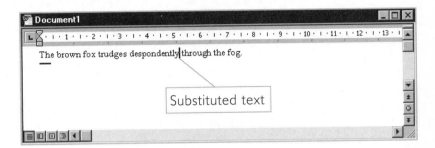

## Adding More Text to the End of the Document

Remember that before adding more text to the end of your document, you must first reposition the insertion point:

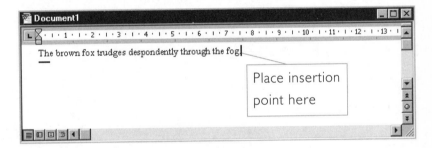

2 Add the text:

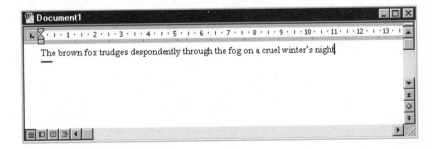

### Insert versus Overtype

At the bottom of the screen, in the Status bar, the letters "OVR" should be greyed out. This indicates that you are in Insert, rather than Overtype mode.

1 Double-click the "OVR" indicator.

The text in the "OVR" indicator will turn black, showing that Overtype mode is selected. In Overtype mode, new text overtypes (replaces) any text to the right of the insertion point, instead of shifting the old text to the right.

2 Position the insertion point somewhere within your text:

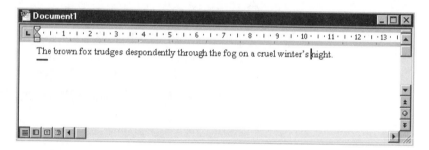

3 Type some new text.

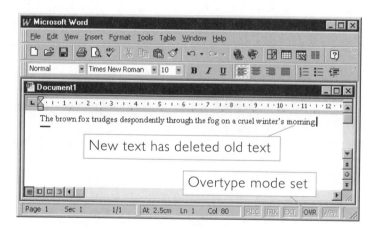

New text has deleted old text

Overtype mode set

4 Double-click once more on the "OVR" indicator to switch back to Insert mode.

## Selecting All the Text in a Document

Choose the "Select All" option from the Edit Menu (or type Control+A).

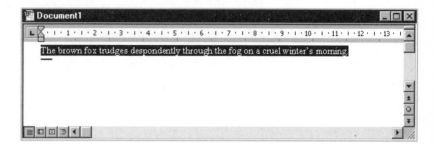

## Changing the Appearance of Text

With all the text selected, open the "Size" pop-up menu from the toolbar, and increase the point size of the text to twice the previous value.

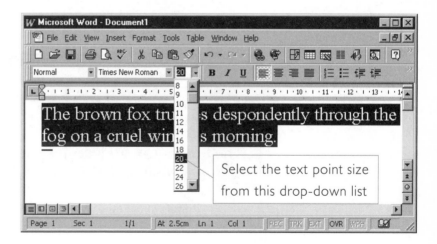

2 Select a single word and use the toolbar to switch on the Bold effect.

*The keyboard shortcut for Bold is Control+Shift+B.*

3 If you want to select text over more than one line, either drag over the area required or click at one end of the selection, then hold down Shift and click at the other end:

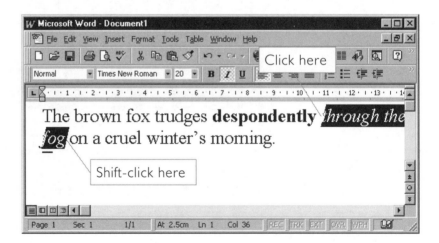

4 You can also select whole lines of text by dragging vertically over the area within the left margin.

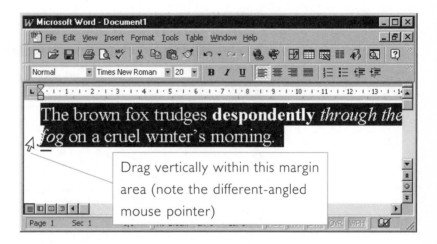

Drag vertically within this margin area (note the different-angled mouse pointer)

5 Alternatively, you can double-click to select a single word, or triple-click to select an entire paragraph.

6 Note if you click an insertion point and then type more text, the new text takes its attributes (appearance) from the previous character:

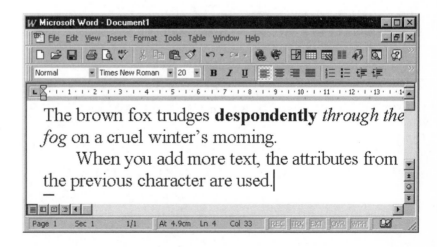

# Saving a Document

The Save icon

To Save your work either choose "Save" from the File menu, or click on the Save icon in the toolbar.

The following dialog box will appear:

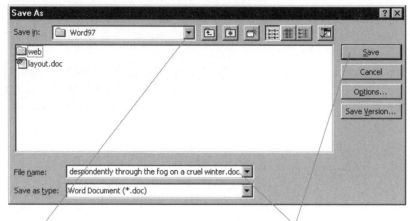

2 If necessary, select the correct drive and folder.

3 Enter the file name and click "Save".

4 If you have finished with the document, choose "Close" from the File menu.

# Opening a Document

*Either*

- Choose "Open" from the File menu or click on the Open icon:

*Or*

- The last few files used are listed in the lower section of the File menu, and can be selected directly.

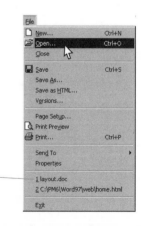

# Print Preview

The Print Preview icon

Before you print a document, you may wish to check it on screen, in order to eliminate any errors that were not spotted at the basic text-proofing stage. Word 97 offers a facility, Print Preview, which shows you all the pages of your document exactly as they will print, with none of the modifications made by the normal Word views. To access this special view, select Print Preview from the File menu, or select the corresponding icon from the Toolbar.

The following screen appears:

*To edit the text in Print Preview, click here – the cursor changes back to its normal text-editing shape – then click in the text and make your changes.*

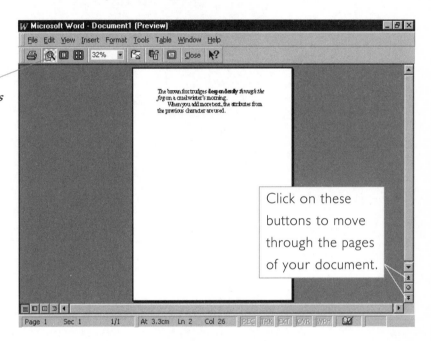

Click on these buttons to move through the pages of your document.

Note that the cursor is initially in the shape of a magnifying glass. To zoom in to a particular area of the page, click over it with the left mouse button; to zoom out, do the same.

If you are satisfied with your document, select Print from the File menu, or click the Print icon: (see the following page). If you want to continue editing it, click Close instead.

# Printing a Document

1 Choose "Print" from the File menu.

The following dialog box will appear:

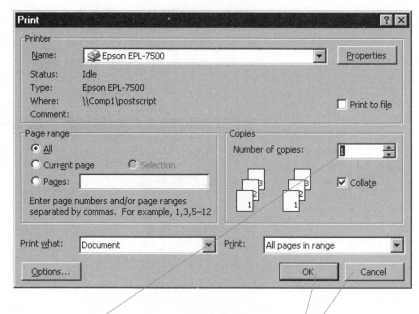

2 Enter the number of copies required.

3 Click "OK" to go ahead, or "Cancel" to abort.

The Print icon

The method detailed above allows you the greatest control over how your document is printed. If, however, you do not need to make any refinements to the printing method, there is a much quicker way to print: simply click the Print icon in the Toolbar. This begins to print immediately, bypassing the Print dialog box and using the default print settings.

# Character-level Formatting

This chapter starts looking at ways in which you can change the appearance of your text. All the effects discussed here apply on a character-by-character basis, as opposed to paragraph-level attributes, which are dealt with in the next chapter.

## Covers

Chapter Three

# Introduction

### What does "Character-level" mean?

Character-level attributes include font name, size, emboldening, underlining plus all sorts of other effects which can be applied to individual characters. If required, every single character could be given different attributes (although this would tend to make your document look a little like a ransom letter).

# Using the Formatting Toolbar

| Select the text which you want to format.

2 Choose the font required from the pop-up menu in the toolbar:

*If you highlight a portion of text, the toolbar will indicate its current formatting options.*

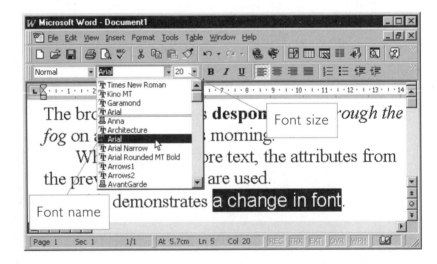

A font is a collection of characters with a particular visual style. Common fonts include:

Times or Times New Roman (useful for main text)
**Arial (useful for headings)**
`Courier (the typewriter font)`

3  Look at the font names in the pop-up list:

The most recently used fonts appear above this line.

TrueType symbol

Printer icon

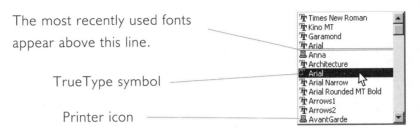

- A printer icon beside the name indicates a printer font. Your machine will use the closest available screen font (which may not match the printed output exactly).

- A double T symbol indicates a TrueType font, which is used for both screen display and printing.

- No symbol beside the font name indicates a screen font. Always check that your printer can reproduce this to a high enough quality.

4  You can use the buttons on this toolbar to add effects such as Bold, Italic, and Underline:

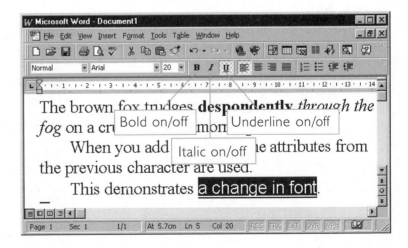

# The Font Dialog Box

This controls all aspects of character-level formatting.

1 Select the text to change.

2 Either choose "Font" from the Format menu, then go to step 4, or click your right mouse button inside the document window.

Right-clicking brings up a pop-up menu that contains options which are relevant to the task in hand. Later you will see that it changes depending on your current context.

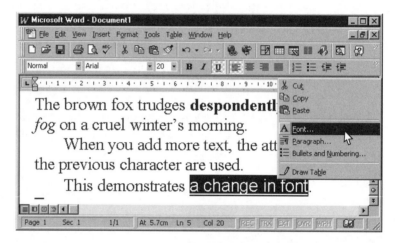

3 Choose "Font".

4 This dialog box appears. Experiment with the different options, noting how they affect the Preview image.

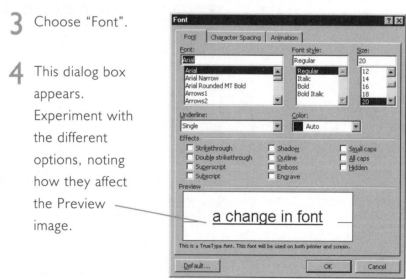

5 Click on the Character Spacing tab.

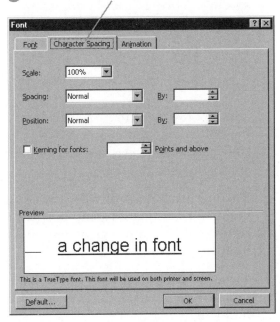

From here you can numerically control the character spacing, the position (for superscript and subscript), and kerning.

6 Click on the Animation tab.

This new feature allows you to enhance text by adding animated effects to it. Of course, these effects are not intended for printed matter, but for on-line documents.

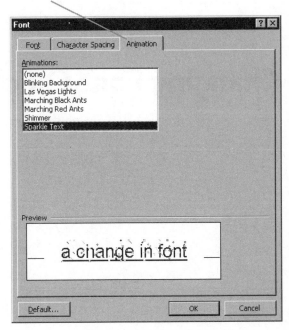

# Kerning

Certain pairs of letters look odd with normal character spacing. Word 97 uses kerning tables, which tell it how much closer together to bring them.

e.g. **To**
**To**

This process of examining each pair of adjacent characters in the document would slow down your machine considerably, so if you activate kerning you should set a threshold of approximately 12 points.

This means that Word will only consider text larger than 12 points for kerning. Spacing in small text is not so noticeable, so this will speed things up without a marked deterioration in quality.

To activate kerning, select the Character Spacing tab of the Font dialog box (see the previous page), then do the following:

1 Switch on the "Kerning for fonts" checkbox.

2 Set the "Points and above" value.

# Changing Font Quickly

1 Select the text.

2 Press Control+Shift+F.

3 Type the first few letters of the font and press the Down Arrow key. You need to type enough letters to distinguish the font name from any others which may be similar.

4 Press Return.

# Paragraph-level Formatting

This chapter looks at ways of manipulating text on a paragraph-by-paragraph basis. It is often tempting to use the space bar to position text on the page, but this quickly leads to problems if text is edited or its attributes are changed. The benefits of alignment, indents and other automatic formatting features are well worth the time it takes to learn how to use these techniques.

## Covers

Chapter Four

# Overview

### What does "Paragraph-level" mean?

Options such as alignment, left and right indents, and space above and below refer to whole paragraphs, i.e. each paragraph has only one set of these attributes.

### Formatting with the Toolbar

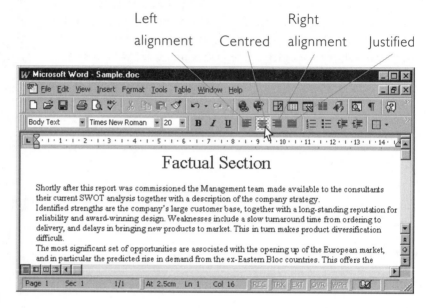

Left alignment    Centred    Right alignment    Justified

*If you are changing just one paragraph you need only click an insertion point somewhere within it. Any change to a paragraph-level attribute will always affect the entire paragraph surrounding the insertion point.*

1  Select the paragraph(s) to format. Remember that a heading is often a single-line paragraph.

2  Choose the form of alignment by clicking on the appropriate tool in the formatting toolbar.

# Forms of Alignment

There are four forms of alignment:

### Left
Text lines up along its left edge, with a ragged right edge.

### Right
Here the text is moved so that the right edge is straight, and the left is ragged.

### Centre
Text is centred between the left and right edges.

### Justification
The text spacing is adjusted so that each line within a paragraph begins and ends in the same position (dictated by the margins and indents), giving a neat and regular appearance. Below is an example of justified text:

*The last line of every justified paragraph is only aligned left, allowing the reader to easily distinguish one paragraph from another.*

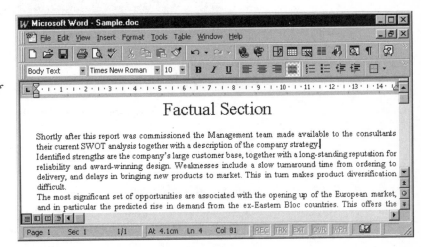

# Bulleted Paragraphs

## Activating Bullets

1 Select the paragraphs to be bulleted.

2 Click on the Bullet icon in the Formatting toolbar...

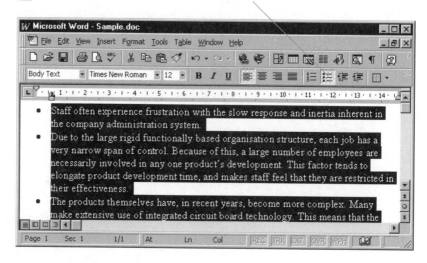

## Removing Bullets

1 If necessary, re-select the bulleted paragraphs.

2 Click on the Bullet icon a second time.

## Automatic Bullets

This is similar to the automatic numbering feature discussed on page 39. If you begin a paragraph with an asterisk, and then enter a carriage return, Word 97 automatically replaces the asterisk with a bullet, and starts the next paragraph with another. When you reach the end of the list that you want bulleted, erase the bullet that has just been created.

# Advanced Bulleting

1 Select the text to be bulleted.

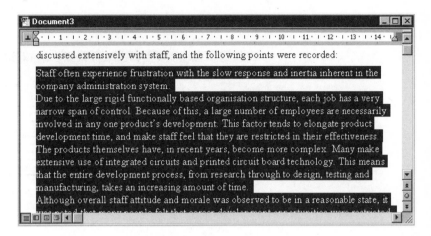

2 Choose "Bullets and Numbering" from the Format menu.

If necessary, click on the "Bulleted" tab.

*You can also select "Bullets and Numbering" from the pop-up menu which appears when you click in the document window with the right mouse button.*

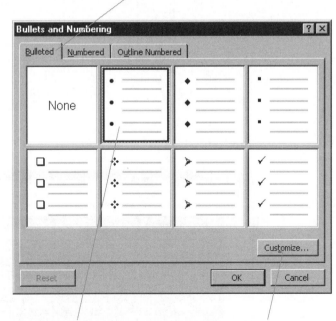

3 Choose the type of bullet text.

4 Click on "Customize" to see further options.

The following dialog box appears:

**5** Choose the required settings. Click on the required bullet...

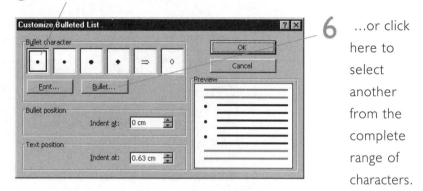

**6** ...or click here to select another from the complete range of characters.

**7** Select the font and character.

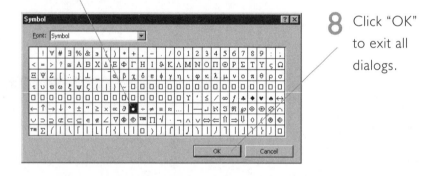

**8** Click "OK" to exit all dialogs.

The selected text is now bulleted:

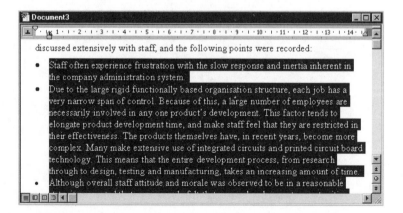

# Numbered Paragraphs

1 Select the paragraphs to be numbered.

2 Click on the Numbering icon in the Formatting toolbar:

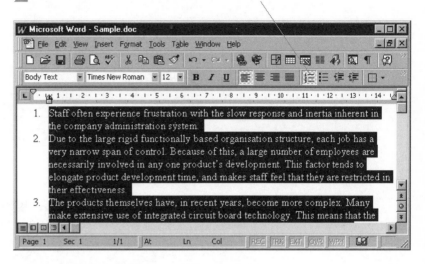

## Removing Numbers

1 If necessary, re-select the numbered paragraphs.

2 Click on the Numbering icon a second time.

## Automatic Numbering

If you begin a paragraph with a number, and then enter a carriage return, Word 97 automatically starts the next paragraph with the next number. When you reach the end of the list that you want numbered, simply erase the number that has just been created.

# Advanced Numbering

1 Select the text to be numbered.

2 Right-click on the selected text, then choose "Bullets and Numbering" from the pop-up menu.

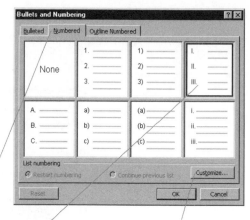

3 Select the "Numbered" tab.

4 Choose a style.

5 Click on "Customize".

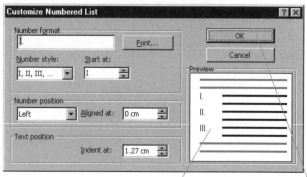

6 Experiment with different settings, referring to the Preview box.

7 Click "OK" to exit all dialog boxes.

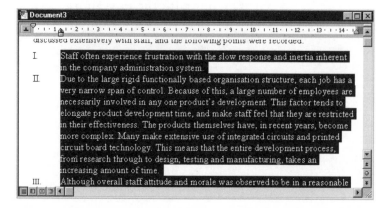

# Outline Numbered Lists

Outline numbered lists contain nested sets of headings and subheadings. Because this function helps you to structure your numbered lists, you are likely to use it differently from the way you would use the normal numbering function discussed on the previous page.

1 With the cursor positioned at the point where you want to begin your multi-level structured list, select "Bullets and Numbering from the Format menu, and choose the Outline Numbered tab.

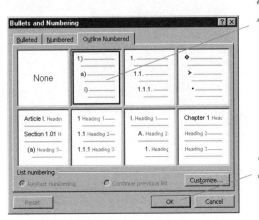

2 Select one of the numbering styles from the top row (i.e., those that don't contain any heading styles.

3 Click OK.

4 In the Word document, enter your list, pressing Return at the end of each element.

5 To place a line at a subordinate level to the one above it, right-click anywhere in the line, and select "Increase Indent". To move a line to a higher level, select "Decrease Indent".

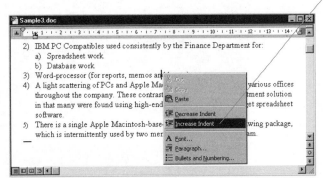

# The Paragraph Dialog Box

This controls all aspects of paragraph-level formatting.

**1** Select the text to be formatted.

**2** Either choose "Paragraph" from the Format menu, or...

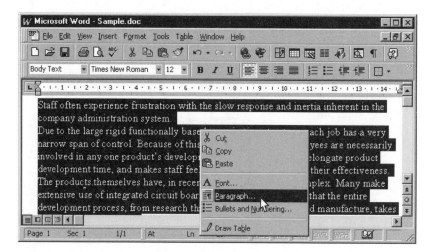

**3** Click your right mouse button somewhere within the document window and select "Paragraph" from the pop-up menu.

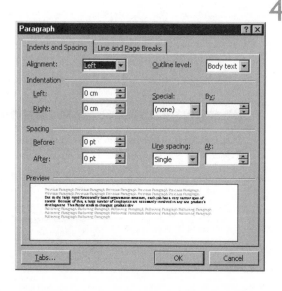

**4** Experiment with the different paragraph controls, checking the results in the preview image. You can adjust the left and right indent, the space above and below a paragraph, or the line spacing within a paragraph.

In the example below, a (vertical) "space before" of 6 points and a special hanging indent of 1.5cm have been set:

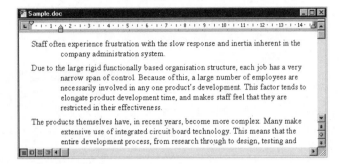

*"Hanging indent" keeps the first line of each paragraph at the left margin, while moving all subsequent lines to the right by a fixed distance.*

In the following example, the line spacing has been changed to "exactly" 16 points. This means that each line in the selected paragraphs will be given exactly 16 points of vertical space regardless of the size of font.

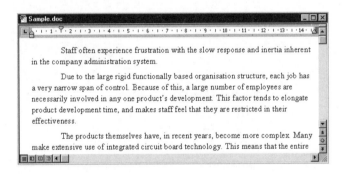

## The Points System of Measurement

This system was introduced firstly in the USA last century, and then adopted by the UK and some European countries.

*72 points is equal to 1 inch.
12 points is equal to the size of normal typewriter text.*

It provides a standard way of measuring the size of type, and often refers to the vertical dimension of characters in a given font. For this reason it is often useful to adjust vertical spacing using points, so that the space between paragraphs uses the same system as the paragraphs themselves.

## The Line and Page Breaks Tab

1 Activate the Paragraph dialog box (either from the Format menu or by clicking in the document window with the right mouse button).

*A widow is a single line of text at the beginning of a paragraph separated from the rest by a page break. An orphan is a similar line at the end of a paragraph. Both widows and orphans look unattractive and should be avoided if possible.*

2 Choose the Line and Page Breaks tab.

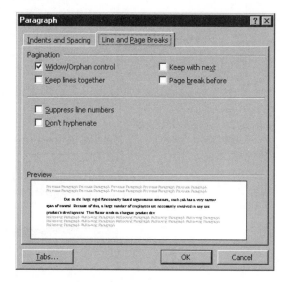

### Widow/Orphan Control
This option instructs Word to automatically move text onto the next page if necessary to prevent widows and orphans occurring.

### Keep Lines Together
Word will move the text so that the paragraph is not broken over two pages.

### Keep With Next
Makes sure that the text is kept with the following paragraph, and not broken over two pages.

### Page Break Before
Forces a new page at the start of the paragraph.

### Suppress Line Numbers
Switches off numbering for this paragraph if line numbers have been used, renumbering the surrounding paragraphs if necessary.

### Don't Hyphenate
Deactivates hyphenation.

# Working with a Document

This chapter helps you to find your way around a document, looking at scrolling, selecting different views and zooming in and out of the page. Additionally we'll look at Cut, Copy and Paste, the Format Painter tool and several other helpful document-formatting features.

## Covers

Chapter Five

# Scrolling

When your text is too large for the document window, you'll need to use one of the following navigation methods:

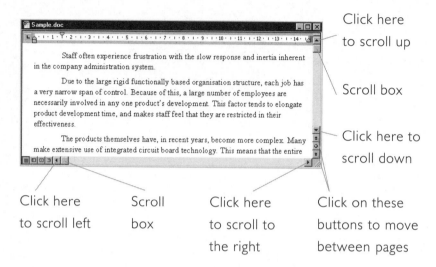

Click here to scroll up

Scroll box

Click here to scroll down

Click here to scroll left

Scroll box

Click here to scroll to the right

Click on these buttons to move between pages

The scroll boxes let you know where you are in a document. For example, when the vertical scroll box is right at the top of the scroll bar, you are looking at the top (the beginning) of the document.

As you scroll down, this box moves down like a lift through a lift shaft.

## Quick Ways to Scroll

- Drag the scroll box directly to a new position.

- Click in the scroll bar to either side of the scroll box. The document will scroll in that direction one screen at a time.

- As you move your insertion point, Word will scroll automatically so that it can always be seen in the document window.

# Zooming

You can use the Zoom pop-up menu to control the level of magnification used by the document window.

Either choose an option from the pop-up menu or enter a new percentage value between 10 and 200.

*If you can afford the space on screen, always maximise both the document window and the Word window itself by clicking on the Maximise button.*

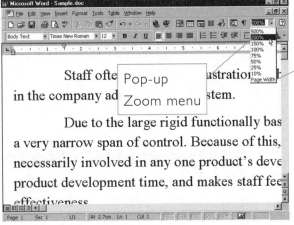

Pop-up Zoom menu

The Page Width option automatically zooms in or out so that the entire width of the page is displayed.

In Page Layout view there are options to display one or more entire pages at a time.

Remember that the more you magnify the page, the more you'll need to scroll. Always try to view the entire horizontal line of text, since frequent horizontal scrolling can be tedious.

## Resizing Windows

*The Restore symbol indicates that a window is already maximised. Click on this to restore the window to its normal size.*

To allocate the greatest possible amount of space to a window, click on the Maximise button. To restore it to its non-maximised size, click on the Restore button.

 Maximise button     Restore button

These are located in a window's top right-hand corner. To adjust the dimensions of a non-maximised window, rest the cursor over one of the window's edges (the cursor changes to a double-headed arrow), then drag the edge to where you want it.

# The Ruler

The ruler gives you a visual account of the tabs and indents used for any selected text.

**1** If the ruler is not visible, activate it by choosing "Ruler" from the View menu.

**2** Select one or more paragraphs of text. Experiment by moving the indent markers:

General left indent marker     First-line indent marker     Default tab stops     Right indent marker

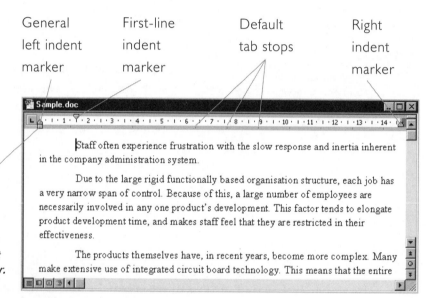

*There is a small square block directly below the left indent marker. Dragging this will move both the left and first line indent markers together.*

## The Paragraph Dialog Box

You can also access these controls numerically from the Paragraph dialog box. See "The Paragraph Dialog Box" in Chapter 4.

# Cut and Paste

1 Select the text to be moved.

2 Right-click on the selected text, then choose "Cut".

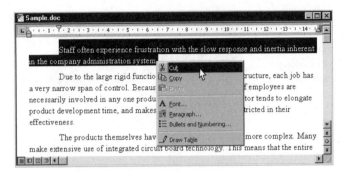

The text is removed and put into the Clipboard.

3 Next position the insertion point at the destination. Holding down the right mouse button, choose "Paste".

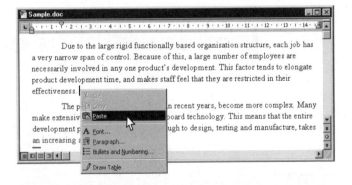

*You can also Cut and Paste using the Edit menu, or the keyboard shortcuts Control+X, Control+V respectively.*

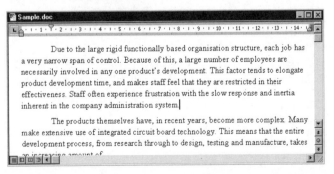

# Copy and Paste

1 Select the text to be copied.

*You can also Copy and Paste using the Edit menu, or the keyboard shortcuts Control +C, Control+V respectively.*

2 Right-click on the selected text, then choose "Copy".

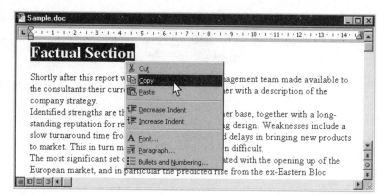

The text is copied into the Clipboard.

*The quickest way to move text is to select it, then drag (from anywhere within the selected area) directly to the new position.*

3 Next, position the insertion point at the destination. Click the right mouse button, then choose "Paste".

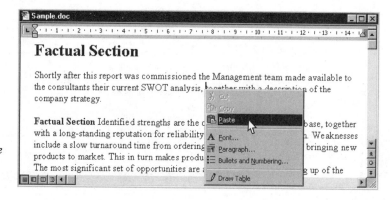

*If you drag the selected area with the Control key held down, then the text will be copied to the new position.*

Once something is in the Clipboard, you can paste it as many times as you like.

# Undo and Redo

- Click the Undo button or type Control+Z to undo the last action.

- Alternatively, open the Undo pop-up menu to review and undo more than one action:

*When undoing or redoing actions using the drop-down menus, drag the cursor down until the actions that you want to undo or redo are highlighted, then click on the menu.*

Undo button        Undo drop-down menu button

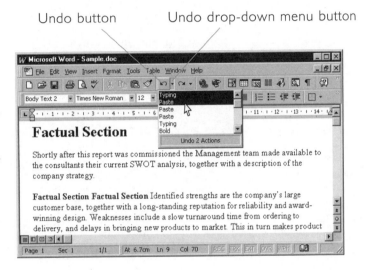

- To redo the undone actions, type Control+Y or use the Redo pop-up menu.

Redo button        Redo drop-down menu button

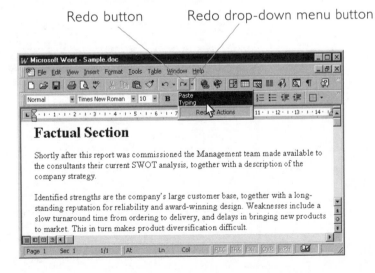

# Page Breaks

Word automatically calculates the position of page breaks. These appear in the document window as a dotted horizontal line (a "soft" page break). However, you can force page breaks, as follows:

> Choose "Break..." from the Insert menu.

The following dialog box appears:

The keyboard shortcut for page break is Control+ Return (or Enter).
To delete a page break, simply select it by clicking in the left margin area and press Delete.

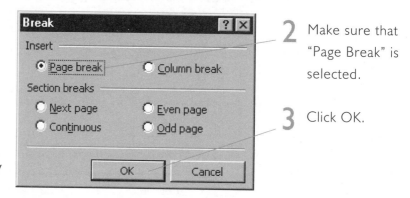

**2** Make sure that "Page Break" is selected.

**3** Click OK.

A "Hard" page break is inserted. The result appears as follows:

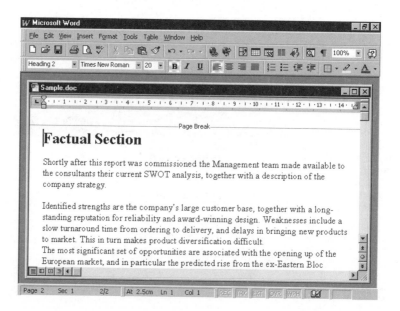

# Defining Sections

1 Click an insertion point part of the way through your document (between paragraphs).

2 Choose "Break" from the Insert menu.

The Break dialog box appears:

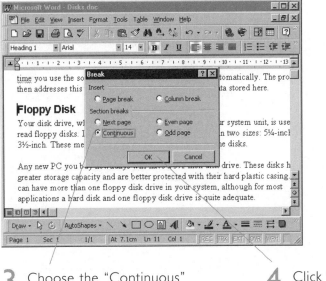

3 Choose the "Continuous" option, under Section Breaks.

4 Click "OK".

The document is now divided into two sections.

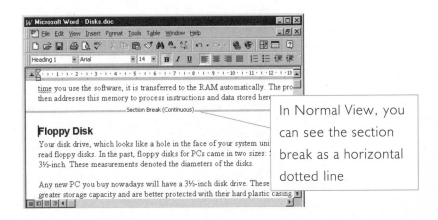

In Normal View, you can see the section break as a horizontal dotted line

# Using Columns with Sections

1 Make sure you are using a document which has been divided into two or more sections.

2 Click the insertion point somewhere in the second section, then choose "Columns" from the Format menu:

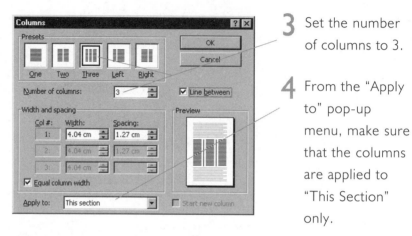

3 Set the number of columns to 3.

4 From the "Apply to" pop-up menu, make sure that the columns are applied to "This Section" only.

5 Click "OK".

You now have a mixed column layout:

*If you drag with the Alt key held down, Word will display the horizontal measurements in the ruler.*

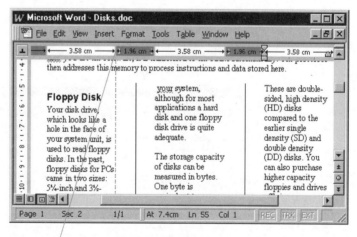

6 You can also adjust the width of columns by dragging the columns' boundary markers in the ruler.

## Column Breaks

You can force text to start in a new column by inserting a hard break.

| Place your insertion point and choose "Break" from the Insert menu.

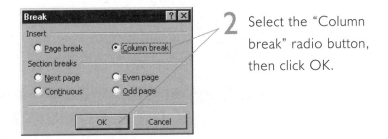

2 Select the "Column break" radio button, then click OK.

This will force the text after the insertion point into a new column.

## Balancing Columns

If there is enough space on the page to accommodate all of your column text, you can balance the columns neatly:

| Click the insertion point at the end of the last column and choose "Break" from the Insert menu.

2 Insert a "Continuous" section break.

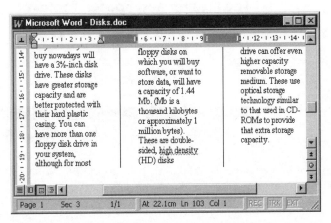

The columns are balanced to within a line or two of each other.

# Headers and Footers

Headers normally appear at the top of every page, footers at the bottom (an example being "Word 97 in easy steps" on this page).

## Creating/Modifying a Header

1    Choose "Header and Footer" from the View menu.

Word will automatically change to Page Layout View. The main page text will be greyed out to let you concentrate on the header. The Header and Footer toolbar will also appear.

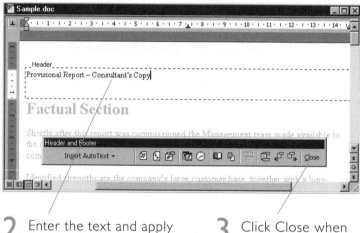

2 Enter the text and apply formatting as required.

3 Click Close when you're finished.

## The Header and Footer Toolbar

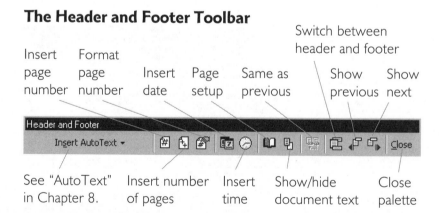

Insert page number

Format page number

Insert date

Page setup

Same as previous

Switch between header and footer

Show previous

Show next

See "AutoText" in Chapter 8.

Insert number of pages

Insert time

Show/hide document text

Close palette

## Creating/Modifying a Footer

1 Click on the "Switch between header and footer" button in the toolbar. This will take you to the footer text.

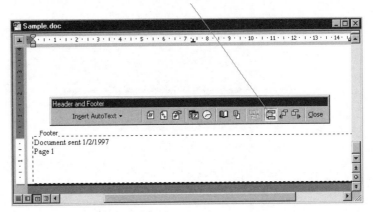

2 Enter the footer text. You can include automatic page numbers, or the current date or time by clicking on the relevant button in the toolbar.

3 Click "Close" when you've finished.

*By default, the header and footer on a page will apply to all remaining pages in the document. You can override this by editing the headers/footers for other pages separately.*

Now the header and footer text is greyed out, and you can edit the main text again. Note that the picture below shows Page Layout View. In Normal View, headers and footers do not appear at all.

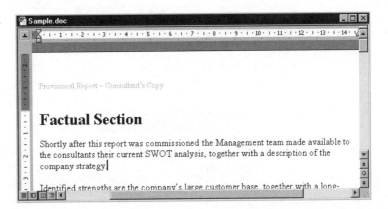

# The Format Painter

This allows you to copy the formatting options from one piece of text to another:

Select the source text and click on the Format Painter icon.

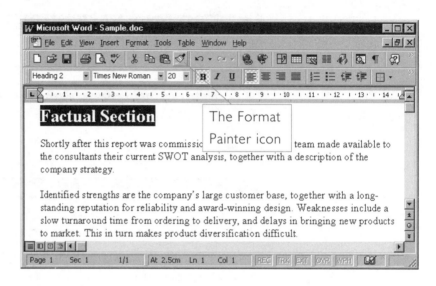

The Format Painter icon

*To copy formatting to more than one destination, simply double-click the Format Painter icon. You can then apply the new formatting to as many pieces of text as you wish. When you've finished, either click back on the icon or press the Escape key.*

2 Now drag across the destination text. The formatting is applied to the new text.

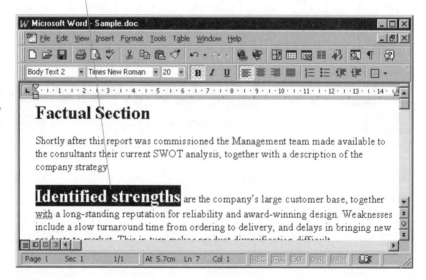

# Document Properties

Windows 95 introduced file names which could be longer (and so more descriptive) than the Spartan eight characters allowed by MS-DOS. Even so, it is useful to record additional information as part of each Word document to help you organise your work, and remember your document's purpose.

| Go to the File menu and choose "Properties".

2 Enter the relevant details. These will be saved along with your document.

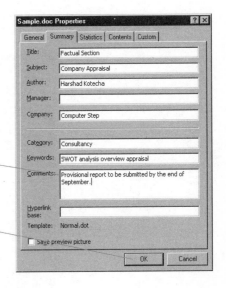

3 Click OK when you're done.

 *The Statistics tab in the Properties dialog will show you useful information about your document.*

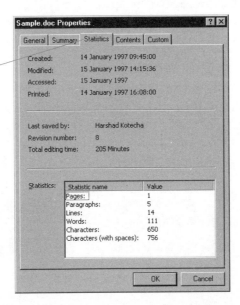

4 When you use the Open document dialog, you can click on the "Advanced" button to tell Word to search on the basis of the information entered in a document's properties.

# The Document Map

The Document Map is a feature new to Word 97, which uses the headings in your document to create an outline of of the document's structure. It appears in a separate pane to the left of the main editing area, and can be used to navigate easily through the document. To display the Document Map, do the following:

1 Click on the Document Map button.

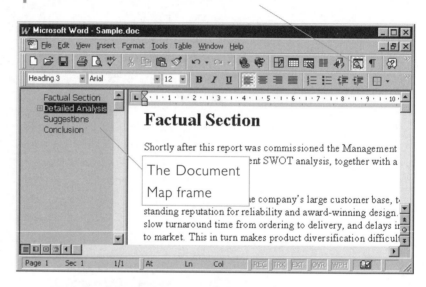

2 To jump to a heading listed in the Document Map, simply click on its entry.

Note that, in the illustration above, the heading "Detailed Analysis" has a small plus-sign next to it. This indicates that there are subheadings beneath it. To display these headings, click on the plus sign:

To collapse the structure to show only the main headings, click on the minus-sign.

The subheadings are now displayed.

# Styles

Styles help you to easily apply a consistent set of formatting commands to main text, headings and other elements of your document.

Once you start using styles, you'll be able to control your document's presentation with the minimum of tedious manual editing.

## Covers

Chapter Six

# Using the Default Styles

A style is a complete collection of type attributes saved under a single name. There are two main benefits to this:

- Your document will have a visual consistency if, for example, all your subheadings look the same.

- You can quickly make drastic but coherent changes to the format of your document by redefining the styles already used by the text.

### Applying a Style

| Select the text.

2 Select a style from the drop-down menu:

You can also use the keyboard shortcut Control+ Shift+S to open the Style drop-down menu. Then type the first few letters of the style, press the down arrow key, and press Return to apply the style.

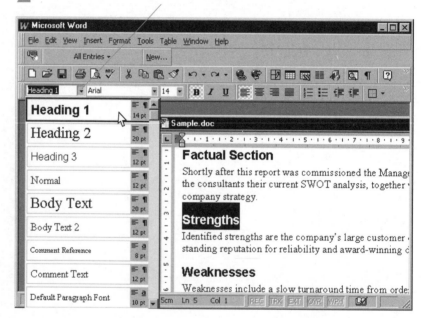

The text has now been set to this style. Whenever you select text on the page, the drop-down menu will indicate which style is currently being used.

By default all text starts off using the style "Normal".

# Editing an Existing Style

1 Select some text in the document which already uses the style to be changed.

2 Use the toolbar and menus as normal to experiment with changes in formatting (see Chapter Three).

3 When you are happy with the changes, reselect the style from the pop-up list:

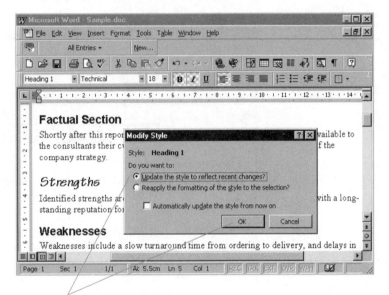

4 In the dialog which appears, make sure the "Update the style..." option is selected and click "OK".

All text in the document using this style will now change automatically...

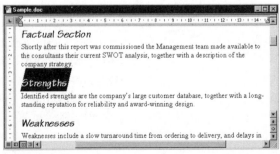

# Creating a New Style

You can easily create a new text style in Word 97, simply by altering existing text, and then entering a name for the new style, which will take these properties:

1 Format the text as normal in the document (see Chapter Three), then select it.

2 When you are happy with its appearance, click on the Style menu box, enter the new style's name, and press Enter:

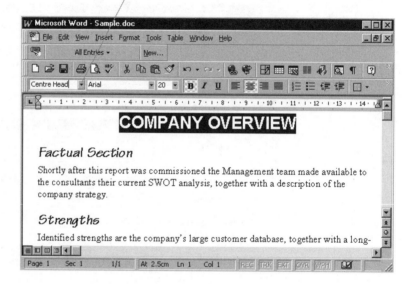

The new style is automatically created, and can now be applied to other text.

## Automatic Style Creation

When you alter the formatting of text, Word 97 can create a new style for you. For example, if you enter a small number of words without punctuation on a single line, apply some changes to the font, size or font effects, and then press Enter, Word will usually assume that this is a new heading style, and create a new style automatically. Thus, if you already have three heading styles, named "Heading 1", "Heading 2", etc., the new style will be named "Heading 4".

# The Style Dialog Box

Word 97 allows you to make most of the style changes you should need from the Formatting toolbar; but the Style dialog allows you to preview potential style changes on a large portion of text, and then to cancel out of the dialog without actually making any of the changes. To open the dialog, do the following:

1 Select Style from the Format menu. The dialog appears:

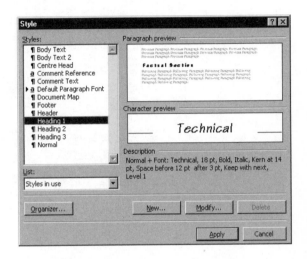

## Creating a New Style Using the Style Dialog Box

1 Click on the "New" button in the Style dialog box (see above).

2 Enter the new style's name.

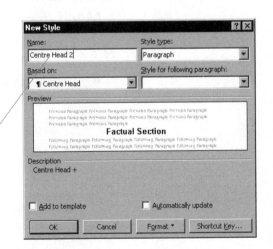

3 See the "Setting the Format" topic on the following page for how to change the new style's properties.

### Setting the Format

| Click on the Format button in the New Style dialog box:

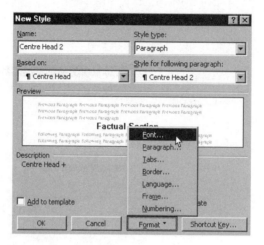

**2** This menu appears, from which you can select the dialogs that control the various properties of the style. Make the appropriate changes, referring to the formatting topics in Chapters Two, Three and Four.

**3** When you have made your changes, click "OK". The new style is added to the list.

### Modifying a Style

| From the Styles dialog box, click on "Modify".

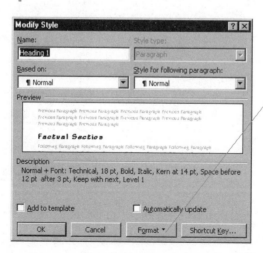

**2** Use the Format button to make the desired changes, then click "OK".

## Setting a Keyboard Shortcut for a Style

1 Click the "Shortcut Key" button in the Modify Style or New Style dialog box.

The Customize Keyboard dialog appears:

*Word tells you if your proposed shortcut key is currently being used for something else. If you go ahead, then your style shortcut will override the previous setting.*

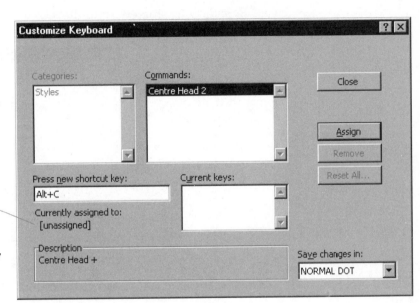

*Most single keystrokes will already be assigned a function, so you will probably need to use a combination of keys, using the Ctrl and/or Alt keys. When you enter the shortcut key combination, all you have to do is press the keys that you want to use: you don't have to type out "Ctrl" or "Alt" in full.*

2 Enter the shortcut key combination for the style and click the "Assign" button. You can repeat this process to add more than one keyboard shortcut for the same style.

3 When you have finished, click the "Close" button to return to the previous dialog box.

# Character-level Styles

Normally styles operate on a paragraph level, i.e. they only apply to whole paragraphs.

To create a character-level style:

**1** Choose "New" from the Style dialog.

**2** Select "Character" from the "Style type" pop-up menu.

**3** Enter a name for the new style here.

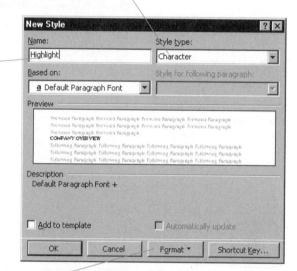

**4** Use the "Format" pop-up to set the character-level attributes.

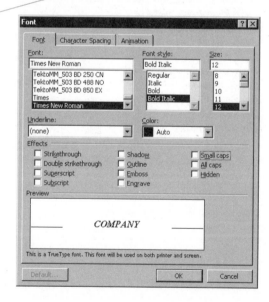

You can now apply your character style to individual words or phrases without affecting the entire surrounding paragraph.

If text already uses a paragraph style, then the character style will override these settings:

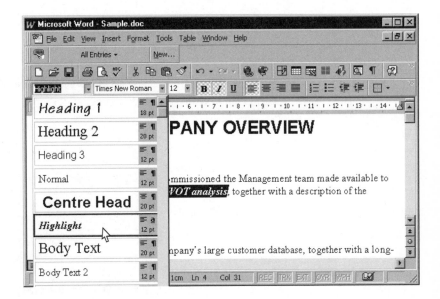

## Identifying Style and Paragraph Names

Character-level style names are labelled in the pop-up list with a. Paragraph styles are labelled with ¶.

# AutoFormat

Word uses a feature called AutoFormat to apply suitable styles automatically to the different parts of your document, without you having to select them. For example, it analyses whether a paragraph seems to be functioning as body text, as a heading, or as part of a list. AutoFormat is turned on by default, but you can change this as follows:

**1** Choose "AutoCorrect from the Tools menu, then select the "AutoFormat As You Type" tab.

**2** Select which formatting changes AutoFormat should make automatically as you enter your text.

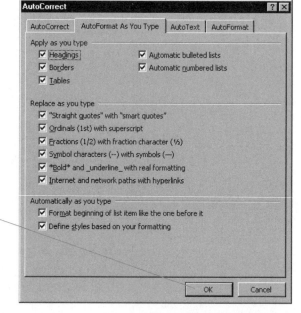

**3** Click OK.

If AutoFormat has been deactivated while you have typed in a document, and you subsequently want to have the document formatted automatically, do the following:

**1** Select AutoFormat from the Format menu.

**2** Tell Word what sort of document this is, then click OK.

# The Style Gallery

When you work on a document, a template is used to tell Word which formatting properties to use for the different character and paragraph styles. You can use the Style Gallery to apply the properties of different templates, to produce an instant overall change to the appearance of your document.

1 Activate the Style Gallery dialog by choosing Style Gallery from the Format menu.

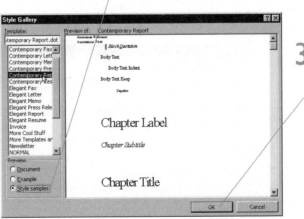

2 Choose a template design, then a preview option. "Document" shows you how your document would look with the proposed style definitions. "Example" shows you an example document demonstrating the different styles.

"Style samples" lists each style name using its own attributes.

3 Click "OK" if you want your document to adopt these new style definitions.

# Displaying Style Names

Sometimes it is useful to see instantly which styles are being used by the paragraphs in your document.

**1** Make sure that Normal View is active (you can set this using the View menu or the icon at the bottom left of the screen).

**2** Choose "Options" from the Tools menu.

**3** Click on the View tab.

**4** Set the "Style area width" to a figure greater than zero.

**5** Click "OK".

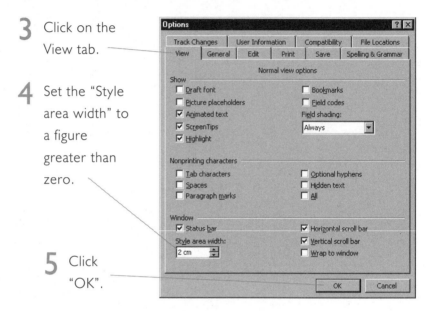

In this example we've used a 2cm margin area in which to list the styles used.

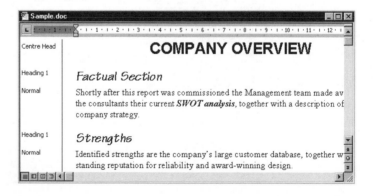

# Tabulation

Text which is laid out with correct and accurate horizontal alignment greatly helps to give a document a professional look.

Effective use of white space, including tabulation, is one of the most important considerations when using a word-processor. This chapter deals with a range of tabulation features and examples.

## Covers

Chapter Seven

# Default Tabulation

The default tab stops are set every half inch. When you press the Tab key, Word automatically moves across the page, stopping when it reaches the next tab stop position.

To see how this works:

1 Make sure that the ¶ button is active.

2 Enter items of text separated by a single tab character.

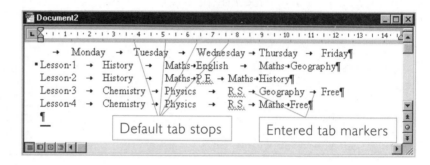

# Creating Your Own Tabulation

1 Select the text.

2 Click in the lower half of the ruler (or the grey bar beneath it) to create a new tab (shaped like an "L") and drag to adjust its position.

New left-aligned tab stop

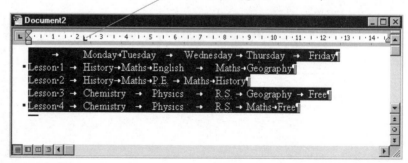

**...cont'd**

*Any new tab stops you create will automatically override the default tabs.*

**3** Repeat this process to create more tab stops.

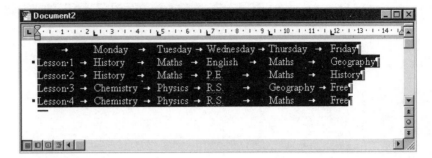

## Deleting Tabs

You can delete your tab stops simply by dragging them downwards out of the ruler.

## Different Types of Tab

So far you've created left-aligned tabs, which cause text to align along its left edge under the tab stop.

*You can move your own tab stops at any time by dragging them within the ruler - but be sure to select the main text first.*

**1** Click the Tab Alignment button once to change to centre tabs.

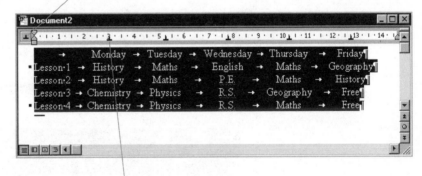

**2** You can now create centred tabs by clicking in the ruler.

As you click on the Tab Alignment button, it cycles between Left, Centre, Right and Decimal alignment.

Here is an example of right-aligned tabs:

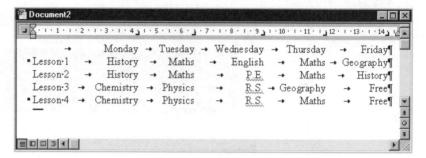

*Tabulation is a paragraph-level attribute. Each paragraph can have its own tab stops if necessary.*

Decimal tabs are used to line up numbers along the decimal point:

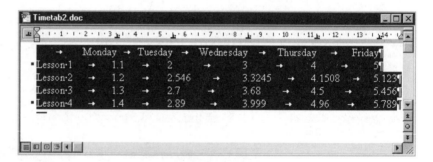

Usually a mixture of different tabs is required:

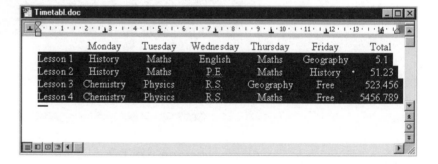

# The Tabs Dialog Box

More options can be found in the Tabs dialog box.

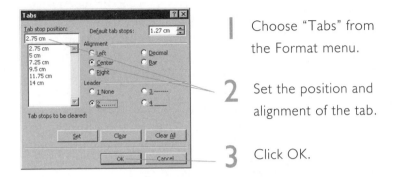

1 Choose "Tabs" from the Format menu.

2 Set the position and alignment of the tab.

3 Click OK.

This example also uses a leader consisting of a row of dots.

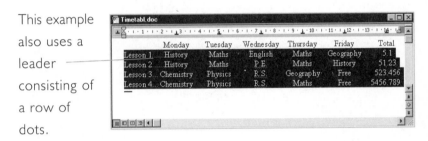

## Bar Tabs

These can only be accessed from the Tabs dialog box, as shown above. Setting a bar tab causes a vertical line to appear in the text at the specified position.

*You can also access the Tabs dialog via the Paragraph dialog.*

Bar tab

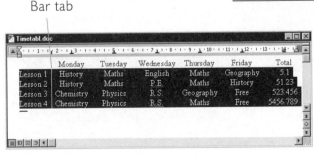

# Using Tabs to Create Tables

The examples used on the preceding pages of this chapter have demonstrated the properties of tabs by using them to create a simple table. However, although this table presents a small amount of information clearly, it contains none of the additional effects that are often used to enhance the presentation of tables: e.g., borders, shaded cells, etc. Word 97 does allow you to create tables that can use such effects as these, using a very simple click-and-drag method (see Chapter 11, "Tables and Charts", for how to do this); but if you have already entered your table data as we have in this chapter, you won't want to type it in all over again. Fortunately, Word allows you to convert such data into true tables very easily:

1   Highlight the data you want to convert, then select "Convert Text to Table" from the Table menu.

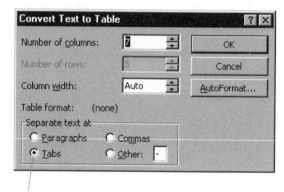

2   If you have separated your columns using tabs, make sure this option is selected, then click OK.

3   The table is created automatically. If the width of a column needs adjusting, rest your cursor over the table column icon to its right, then click and drag it to where you want it.

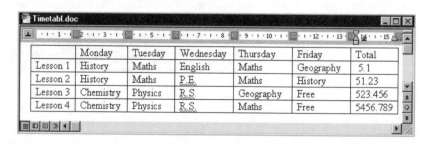

# Automatic Features

Word has many automatic features which will operate on selected text or a complete document. This chapter looks at many of these, including search and replace tools and facilities for correction of spelling and grammar.

## Covers

# Chapter Eight

# Find and Replace

## Finding Text

Word can be instructed to search through your document for particular words, groups of characters, or formatting attributes.

1 Choose "Find" from the Edit menu, or type Control+F.

*Using the checkboxes in the centre of the dialog, you can set the Find dialog to look for text in a particular case, for whole words (rather than groups of letters), to use wildcard searching, or phonetic matching. If these checkboxes are not displayed, click the button labelled "Less" here, which will instead read "More".*

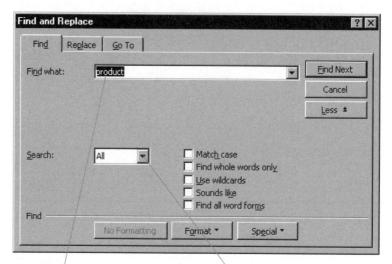

2 Enter your search text here.

3 Set the search direction, either from the insertion point downwards, upwards or throughout the entire document.

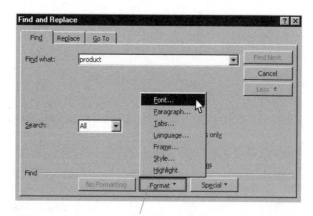

4 If you want to make a search based on attributes, open the Format pop-up menu, and choose the relevant option(s).

In this example we're searching for Times New Roman 12-point text:

5 Click "OK" to
return to the Find
dialog, then click
on the Find button
to start the search.

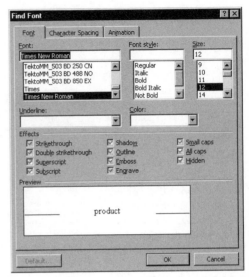

Word highlights the first instance of text matching your search criteria:

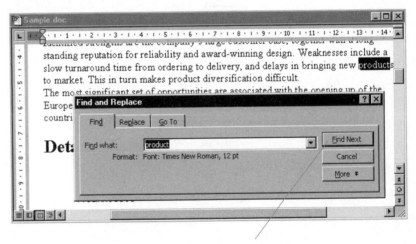

6 Click on Find Next to continue searching for subsequent instances of text matching the same search criteria.

## Replacing Text

Once you have found an instance of the text you are searching for, you can choose to replace it with some different text.

1 Click on the Replace tab.    2 Enter the "Replace with" text.

*To open the Find and Replace dialog with the Replace tab active, you can choose Replace from the Edit menu, or type Control+H. You can then enter the "Find what" text here before continuing with step 2. However, if you want to search for text with a particular format, you'll have to use the Find tab.*

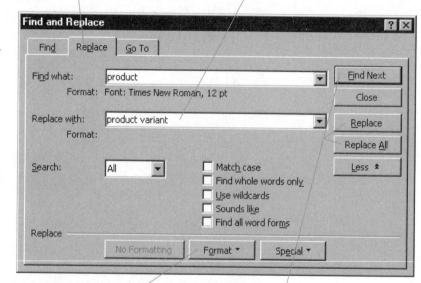

3 If you wish to replace the search text with text that has different format attributes, click here and choose the relevant options.

4 Click Replace to change just this instance of the target text, Replace All to change every instance in the document, or Find Next to skip to the next instance.

5 When you're done, click Close.

# Special Characters

You can use the "Special" pop-up menu in the Find and Replace tabs to easily insert the keyboard codes for special characters. In this example we're looking for two consecutive paragraph marks, and replacing them with a single paragraph marks.

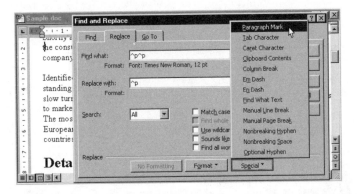

## Wildcards

If you want to search not for a specific piece of text, but for text that follows a certain pattern, select the "Use wildcards" checkbox before clicking the "Special" button. You will then find that "Special" pop-up menu contains some extra entries. For example, to search for words that follow the pattern "g?ve" (where "?" represents any single character), you would do the following:

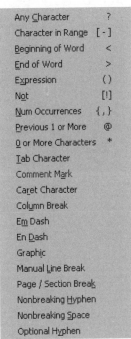

1 Enter the letter "g" in the "Find what" box.

2 Click the "Special" button and select "Any Character" from the menu.

3 Enter the letters "ve".

This search will highlight all words like "give", "gave", and (if you don't have the "Find whole words only" checkbox selected) words like "given", too.

Another very useful wildcard feature available from the "Special" menu is the "Character in Range" function. This allows you to search for numbers or letters in any range you specify. For example, to search for references to years between 1991 and 1997, make sure that the "Use wildcards" checkbox is selected, then do the following:

1 In the "Find what" box, enter "199"

2 Click on the "Special" button and select "Character in Range" from the menu. The text "[-]" will be inserted.

3 Edit the contents of the "Find what" box so that it now reads "199[1-7]".

# Spelling and Grammar Checking

Word allows you to check your spelling and grammar in two ways: either from a special dialog, or on the fly. The dialog is used as follows.

1 If you don't want to spell check your entire document, then select only the text you require.

*The shortcut key for Spelling and Grammar Checking is F7.*

2 Choose "Spelling and Grammar" from the Tools menu, or click on the corresponding icon:

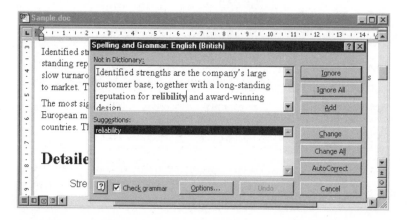

Word 97 highlights spelling mistakes in red, and possible grammatical problems in green.

**3** When a suspect word or phrase is found, you can:

- Click "Change" to replace it with Word's suggestion.
- Select another entry from the list of suggestions, and click "Change".
- Enter your own correction and click "Change".
- Click "Ignore" if the word or phrase is in fact correct.

**4** If you enter your own spelling correction and would like the word to be added to the dictionary, click the "Add" button.

*You can make Word change or ignore all instances of the current text by clicking "Ignore All" or "Change All".*

**5** You can change the dictionary file by selecting from the "Add words to" pop-up menu.

**6** Clicking the "Options" button takes you to the "Spelling & Grammar" options dialog box:

*You can also access the Spelling & Grammar options as a tab of the main options dialog: select Options from the Tools menu.*

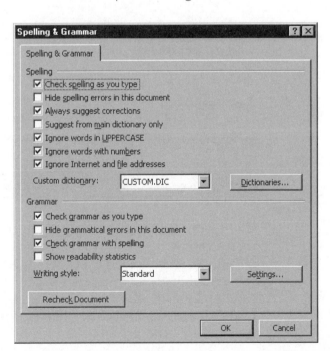

## Readability Statistics

It is possible to make Word 97 display readability statistics for your document, after it has finished performing a Spelling and Grammar check.

1 Select Options from the Tools menu, and choose the Spelling and Grammar tab (illustrated on page 85).

2 Make sure that the "Show readability statistics" checkbox is checked, then click OK.

After you have performed a Spelling and Grammar check, this dialog is displayed:

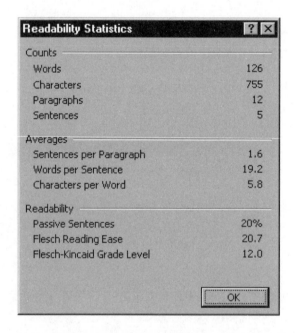

Unfortunately no one has, as yet, figured out a way of automatically analysing the boredom level of a document. This is one job still left to us lucky humans.

The Flesch Reading Ease value is in the range 0...100, increasing with ease of reading. Standard text rates between 60 and 70. The Grade Level values give an indication as to the school grade appropriate for your text. For example, a level of 3 means that it would be understandable by someone in the third grade or below. Standard text normally weighs in between 7 and 8.

## Checking on-the-fly

While the dialog-box method of checking your spelling and grammar offers you the greatest amount of control over exactly how the checking is done, Word 97 can check your grammar and spelling automatically, as you type it, and highlight any problems it finds on the page. Consider the following example:

*Both the Spelling and the Grammar pop-up menus offer a quick route to the full Spelling and Grammar dialog box: simply select the bottom entry, marked with* ✓ABC .

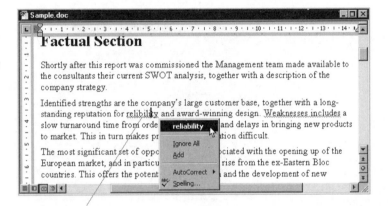

This spelling mistake is underlined in red. To correct it, right-click on it, then select the correct suggested word from the pop-up menu. If the suggestion is not suitable, attempt to correct it yourself, then see if it is still flagged.

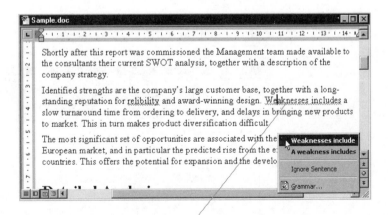

This grammar mistake is underlined in green. Right-click on it, then select the correct suggestion from the menu.

# Word Count

Word provides a quick and easy way of counting the number of words in your document:

1 To count the words in one area only, select it in the normal way – otherwise the entire document will be scanned.

2 Choose "Word Count" from the Tools menu:

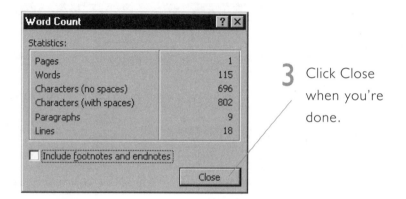

3 Click Close when you're done.

# Thesaurus

If you need to search for a word's synonyms (i.e., words closely related in meaning), you can use Word's built-in Thesaurus.

1 Select the word to be used.

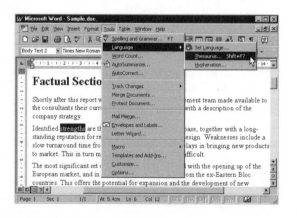

2 Press Shift+F7 or choose Language> Thesaurus from the Tools menu...

The Thesaurus dialog box appears:

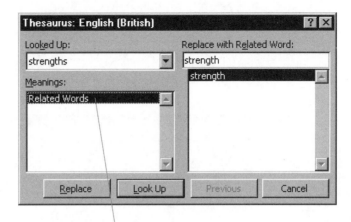

**3** Double-click here to search for the related words.

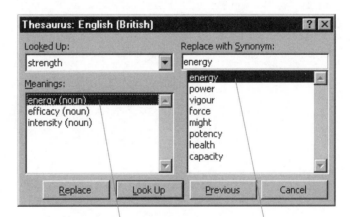

*If none of the words you see listed in the Synonyms pane at step 5 is suitable, try clicking on another entry in the Meanings pane. Alternatively, double-click on one of the words in the Synonyms pane to see the synonyms stored for that word. You can continue in this manner indefinitely.*

**4** The different possible categories of meanings related to your word are listed in this pane. Click on whichever best summarises the meaning you are aiming for...

**5** ...to see the relevant synonyms listed here. If one of these is suitable, click on it, then click the Replace button to change the word in your document.

# AutoCorrect

Often, the same spelling or typing mistakes are made again and again. You can instruct Word to substitute the correction automatically :

> **1** Choose AutoCorrect from the Tools menu, and make sure that this tab is selected.

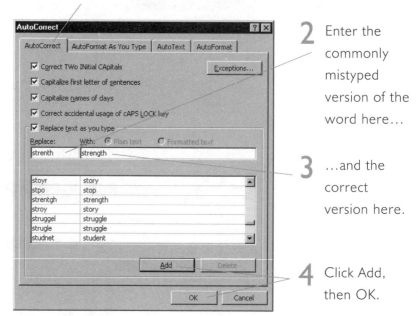

> **2** Enter the commonly mistyped version of the word here...

> **3** ...and the correct version here.

> **4** Click Add, then OK.

If you type the error now, Word spots it and substitutes the correct word automatically, instead of merely flagging it as a possible spelling mistake:

| Identified strenhs | ... | Identified strengths |
|---|---|---|
| *original text typed* | | *corrected by Word* |

You can now continue through the rest of your life completely unaware that you are consistently failing to spell correctly.

# AutoText

This is a less automatic version of AutoCorrect, and is useful for setting up your own abbreviations.

If you find that you often need to type the same text, then it would be worth setting up an AutoText entry:

## Creating an AutoText Entry

**1** Type the text and select it.

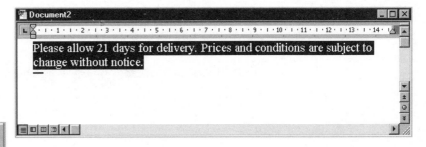

*You can also use the AutoText toolbar button.*

*If it isn't visible, you can display it by checking the AutoText entry in the View>Toolbars menu.*

**2** Choose AutoCorrect from the Tools menu and select the AutoText tab.

**3** Edit the entry in this box to the abbreviation you require.

**4** Click "OK".

The selected text is automatically inserted into the "Selection" area of the AutoText dialog box.

### Using AutoText

*You can also insert AutoText by selecting it from the AutoText tab of the Tools> AutoCorrect dialog box.*

1  Simply type the abbreviation:

The first few words of the stored AutoText entry appear here.

2  Press Enter or F3 to replace the abbreviation with the full text.

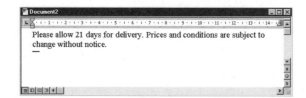

# The Spike

The Spike is a temporary piece of AutoText which can be added to with a single key command.

### Creating a Spike

1  Select some text and type Control+F3.

The text disappears. It has been impaled on the Spike.

2  Repeat the process with a second piece of text.

You can repeat this more times if necessary. Each time you press Control+F3 any selected text is put onto the Spike.

3  Finally, place the insertion point at the destination for the text and press Control+Shift+F3.

The text is pulled off the Spike and placed back into the document.

# AutoComplete

AutoComplete is somewhat akin to AutoText, in that it offers suggestions for the completion of words or phrases that you only need to begin typing. However, while AutoText uses a list of commonly used phrases which have first to be recorded, AutoComplete offers to fill in other sorts of text which can be worked out from the context. For example, AutoComplete can enter:

- the current date

- your name

- your company's name

- any day of the week

- any month

Begin to type in one of the words or phrases listed above (here we're entering today's date).

 *If Auto-Complete doesn't appear to be functioning, choose AutoCorrect from the Tools menu, select the AutoText tab, and make sure there is a tick in the checkbox labelled "Show AutoComplete tip for AutoText and dates".*

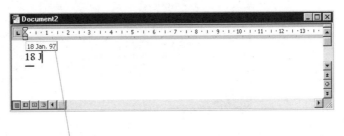

AutoComplete offers to fill in the whole of today's date.

2 To fill in the whole date, simply press Enter or F3.

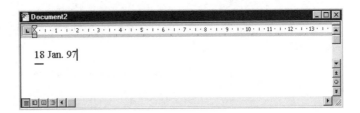

# AutoSummarize

This feature, new to Word 97, uses complex procedures to analyse a document and determine which sentences are likely to carry the document's most significant, salient points. It does this by calculating which words and phrases in the document are used most often. The resulting analysis can then be presented in several different ways.

To use AutoSummarize, do the following:

1 Open the document you want to summarize, then choose AutoSummarize from the Tools menu. The following dialog box appears:

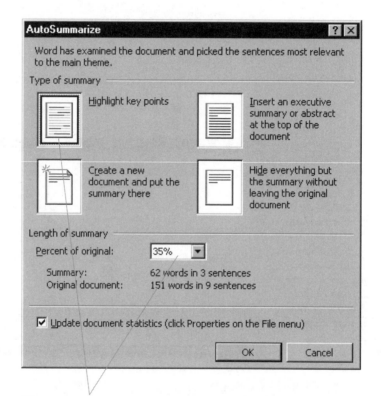

2 Select the way you want to present the summary, and the summary's level of detail, then click OK.

If the "Highlight key points" option is selected, the whole document is displayed, with the most significant points highlighted. Perform any of the following steps, as appropriate:

3 Click here to toggle between displaying the whole text with the summary highlighted, or the summary only.

4 Click here to increase or decrease the summary's level of detail – i.e., the percentage of the document that is highlighted.

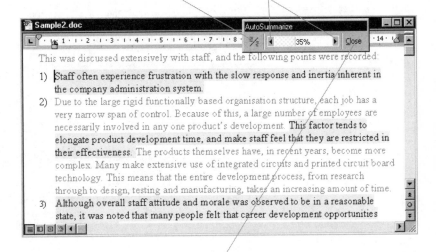

5 Click Close to shut down the AutoSummarize control palette and return to the normal document view.

In this example, Word appears to have determined that the word "staff" is used very regularly in this document, and has highlighted most of the sentences containing it.

# Hyphenation

1 You can change the hyphenation options for your document by choosing Tools>Language>Hyphenation:

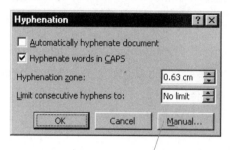

2 If you click on the "Manual" button you can review hyphenation manually throughout your document:

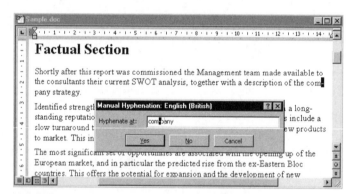

*You can also override hyphen-ation for individual paragraphs by selecting the "Don't hyphenate" checkbox in the Line and Page Breaks tab of the Paragraph dialog box (choose "Paragraph" from the "Format" menu).*

# Templates and Wizards

Templates act as blueprints for standard types of document which you would need to use again and again. Examples may be standard memos, reports, letters or faxes. A Wizard is a "live" document which guides you through its own design.

This chapter shows you how to use templates and Wizards, customise a template for your own purposes, or create a new template.

## Covers

**Chapter Nine**

# Using Templates

A template contains a range of settings to be used as a
starting point for a new document.

## The Normal Template

Choose "New" from the File menu:

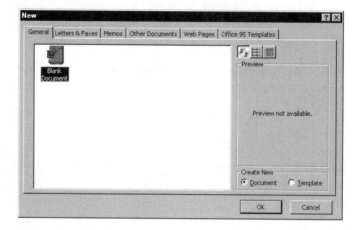

Word lists the templates available. Often you'll use the
simple "Blank Document" template.

2 Click on the other tabs to see more available templates.

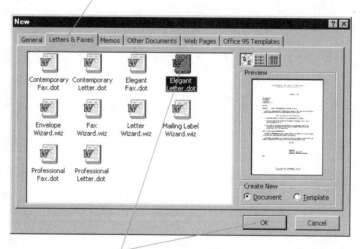

3 Select the template you want to use and click "OK".

# Form Templates

1 Choose "New" from the File menu.

2 Select the Templates tab.

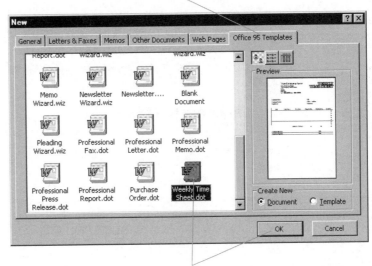

3 Click on "Weekly Time Sheet.dot" and click "OK".

## Form Filling

"Weekly Time Sheet.dot" contains a complete design for a weekly time sheet form. Forms normally contain fields, which can be easily filled in or edited without disturbing the surrounding text.

Use normal editing methods to enter or change the text in a field.

 *Press the Tab key to move on to the next field; press Shift+Tab to move back to the previous field.*

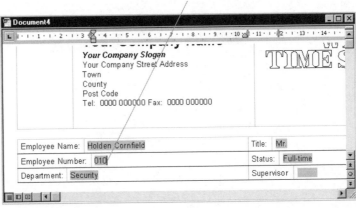

Note that most of the menu options are greyed out, and that you cannot edit the main text in the document. You're restricted to editing the fields, saving and printing.

Provided the template is set exactly the way you want, this allows you to produce forms easily, without being distracted by Word's vast array of features and controls. However, if you want to change the main text provided by the template, you can do so quite easily...

## Changing the Form

To be able to edit the whole of the document, do the following:

1   Go to the Tools menu and choose "Unprotect Document".

2   You can now fully edit the document, adapting it to your own ends:

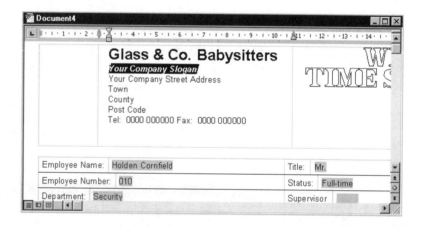

# Template Defaults

Defaults are settings which are used initially when you create a new document or add new text. To change the defaults for a template, do the following with a template open:

1 Open the Font dialog box from the Format menu.

2 Choose your required settings and then click on the "Default" button.

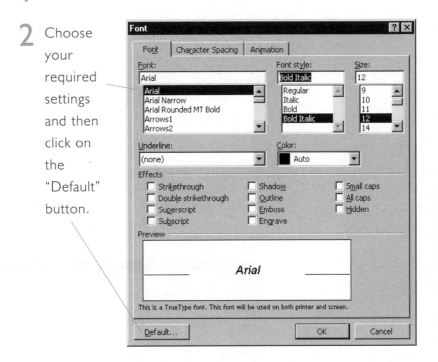

The following dialog appears:

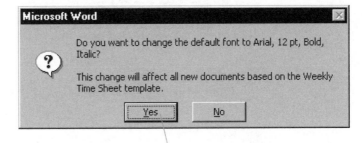

3 If you click "Yes", the font information will be saved into the currently used template document.

# Setting Up a New Template

Any document can be saved as a template, but in this example we'll return to the form from earlier on. With the document open, do the following:

1 Select "Protect Document" from the Tools menu.

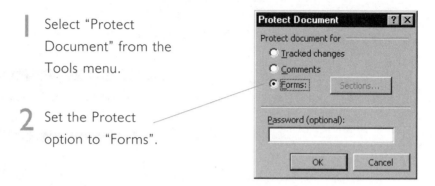

2 Set the Protect option to "Forms".

Note that you only need to do this if the template is to be used as a form.

3 Choose "Save As" from the File menu:

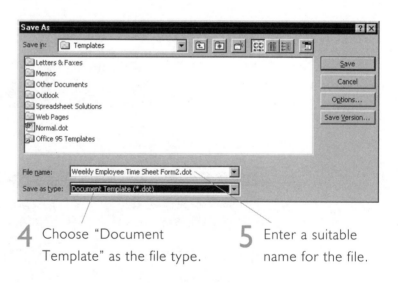

4 Choose "Document Template" as the file type.

5 Enter a suitable name for the file.

6 Click Save.

The document will automatically be saved with a .DOT extension within Word's Templates folder.

# Changing Styles in a Template

When you open a document, Word uses the styles built into the template selected.

As we saw earlier, you can alter these styles for individual documents using the "Style" dialog:

1 Select "Style" from the Format menu.

2 Click on the Modify button to display the following dialog:

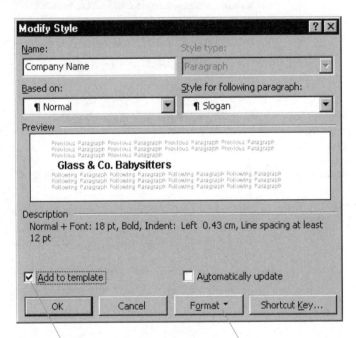

*If you record a style change to the "Blank Document" or "Normal" template, this will affect most new documents.*

4 To copy a style change back into the template itself, make sure the "Add to Template" box is checked.

3 Make any appropriate changes using the dialogs that can be selected from the Format button pop-up menu.

5 Click OK.

# The Templates and Add-ins Dialog

Word always keeps track of the template used to create a document. It is possible to change this even after you've started work:

1 If necessary, unprotect your document (Tools menu).

2 Choose "Templates" from the Tools menu.

*You can use the "Add" button to make available styles stored in other templates. Any templates listed in the "Global" box are always available.*

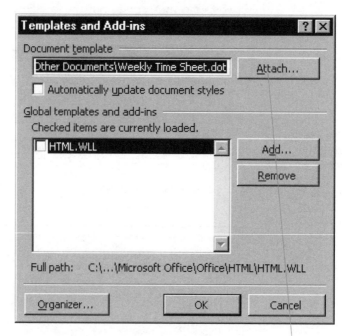

3 Use the "Attach" button to attach a new template. If you select "Automatically Update Document Styles" then the Styles from the new template will be reapplied to the document text.

4 Click OK when you're done.

# Wizards

A Wizard is a sort of "intelligent" template: it helps you design and build a document by asking you a series of questions, which you answer either by selecting from a choice of radio buttons, or by entering text in a box.

## An Example

1 Choose "New" from the File menu, then select this tab.

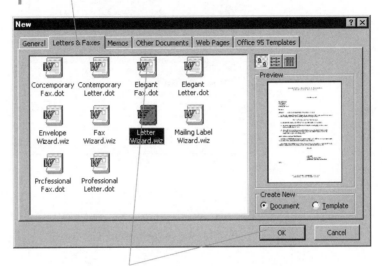

2 Select the "Letter Wizard" icon, then click OK.

3 Tell the Assistant whether or not this letter is for a mailing list.

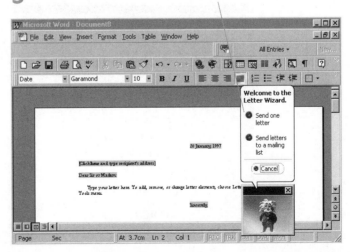

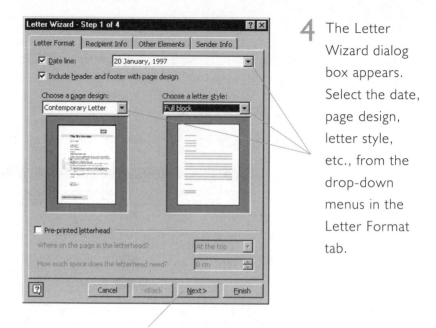

4 The Letter Wizard dialog box appears. Select the date, page design, letter style, etc., from the drop-down menus in the Letter Format tab.

5 When you've finished entering information into this tab, click "Next" to move to the next tab, and enter the appropriate information. Repeat this for all four tabs, then click "Finish".

The Wizard now produces your letter, with many of the main elements already inserted:

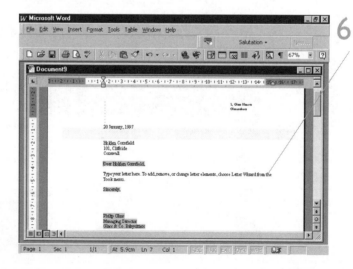

6 Amend the text as you would any normal document.

# Graphical Features

Although not a full-blown graphics package, Word contains a comprehensive collection of clip art as well as a respectable range of graphical editing features. This chapter takes you through the processes involved with incorporating pictures and illustrations into your document.

## Covers

Chapter Ten

# Inserting Clip Art

Word 97 has its own folder of clip art illustrations.

1 Click the insertion point at the destination for the graphic.

2 If most of your clip art is on your Word or Office CD-ROM, put the CD in the drive and choose Insert>Picture>From File.

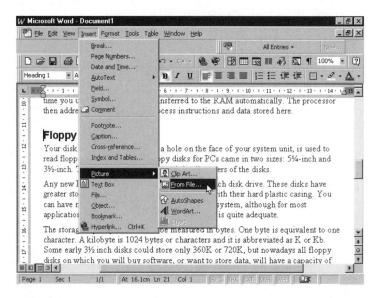

3 Locate the file you require and click "Insert".

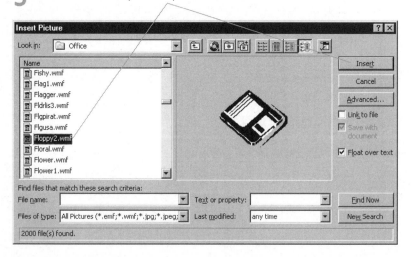

The picture is inserted into the document:

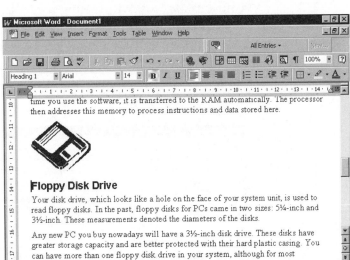

## Types of Graphic File

Word can import many types of graphic file format. WMF, CGM, WPG, DRW, EPS and PCT files normally contain Draw-type objects which can be scaled up or down with no loss in quality, because they are stored as vectors – mathematical objects.

On the other hand BMP, PCX, TIF and GIF files are bitmapped: the image is stored as a structure of tiny dots/ blocks. Be careful not to enlarge these pictures too much, or the dots will become very noticeable, causing a marked deterioration in quality.

# Manipulating Graphics

When you insert a graphic into Word and click on it with
your cursor, you will see eight blocks appear around it: one
at each corner, and one at the middle of each side. These are
the graphic's control handles, which can be used to change
its dimensions.

1   Click on the graphic to make its handles appear.

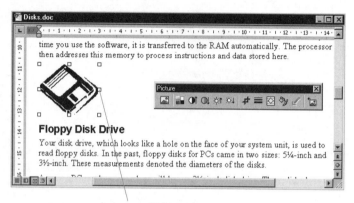

2   Drag on a handle to resize the picture.

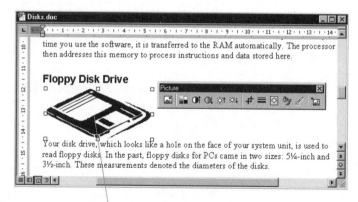

3   Drag anywhere within the object to move it to a new
position.

Note that the graphic is treated like a text item, so when you
drag it to a new position, the surrounding text moves to
make room.

# The Picture Toolbar

The Picture toolbar appears when you insert a picture into a Word document, and provides an easy way of making a wide range of changes to your pictures. It can be used for the following functions:

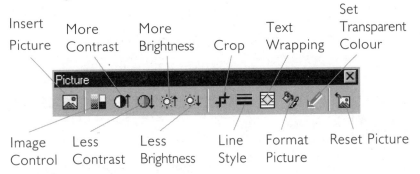

Insert Picture • More Contrast • More Brightness • Crop • Text Wrapping • Set Transparent Colour • Image Control • Less Contrast • Less Brightness • Line Style • Format Picture • Reset Picture

# Cropping a Picture

If you want to display only part of an image in your Word document, you should crop it. This cuts away a part of the picture from any of its four sides. To do this you should use the Crop tool:

*Cropping is non-destructive. This means that you can restore the rest of the picture by dragging the edges back with the Crop tool, or by clicking on the Reset Picture icon.*

1 Select the image

2 Click on the Crop icon in the Picture toolbar

The Reset Picture icon

3 Rest your cursor over any of the picture's control handles, then drag the edges to where you want them.

# Editing an Imported Picture

Most normal clip art pictures that you import will be in vector format (they'll usually have the .WMF extension), which means that they can be broken down into simple, individual elements which can be edited separately. To edit a vector clip art image, simply do the following:

**1** Double-click on the image in your Word document. A new picture window opens:

*If you extend the picture beyond its normal bounding rectangle, click this button to reset the picture boundary. This also applies if you reduce it in size.*

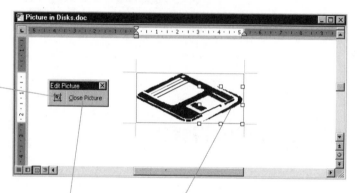

**3** When you have finished, click here to close the picture window.

**2** You will now find that the clip art object is in fact composed of several different objects, which can be selected individually. Click on one, then try stretching or deleting it.

Here, the object that represented the floppy disk's shadow has been deleted.

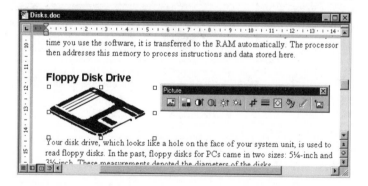

# Wrapping Text Around Graphics

When a graphic is inserted into a Word document, it is placed into the text by default as a simple object, on a new line. However, you can very easily change this, so that text wraps around the image in any of a number of ways:

1 Select the picture.

2 Click on the Text Wrapping icon in the Picture toolbar, and select how you want the text to wrap around the image.

*If the Picture toolbar is not visible, select Toolbars from the View menu, and check the Picture heading.*

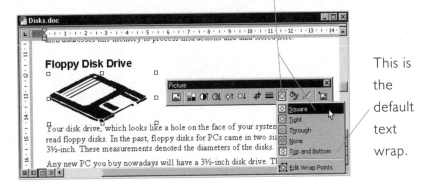

This is the default text wrap.

The text now wraps around the image. This is "Square" wrap: the text wraps around a rectangular area that borders the graphic.

# The Format Picture Dialog

From here you can numerically change all the properties of a graphic, including its size, position, text-wrap properties and crop parameters.

Select the picture.

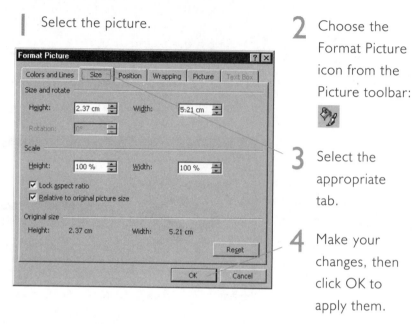

2 Choose the Format Picture icon from the Picture toolbar:

3 Select the appropriate tab.

4 Make your changes, then click OK to apply them.

# The Drawing Toolbar

When working with graphics in Word 97, you are not limited to using ready-made clip art; you can create your own drawings using Word's Drawing toolbar.

 *The draw menu, which is revealed by clicking here, contains many other drawing-related commands.*

To display the Drawing toolbar, click on the Drawing icon in the Standard toolbar, or select View>Toolbars>Drawing:

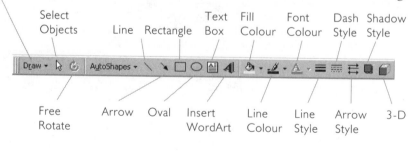

Select Objects — Line — Rectangle — Text Box — Fill Colour — Font Colour — Dash Style — Shadow Style

Free Rotate — Arrow — Oval — Insert WordArt — Line Colour — Line Style — Arrow Style — 3-D

# Creating Shapes

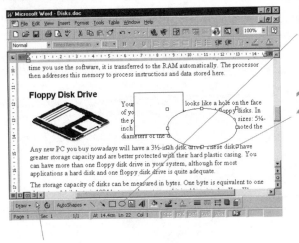

1 Select the appropriate shape tool.

2 Click and drag within the document to create the shape. For lines, drag from one end-point to the other; for boxes and ovals drag diagonally from one corner to the other.

3 Click on a shape with the pointer to select it. Then you can drag it to another location, or resize it by dragging directly on one of its handles.

# Lines and Fills

Click on a shape then use the Fill and Line pop-up menus to select colour, shading and line patterns.

*These properties can also be changed using the Format AutoShape dialog box: right-click on a shape, then select Format AutoShape from the pop-up menu.*

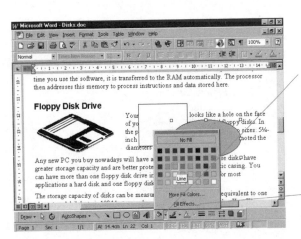

Click on the arrow to the right of the icon to produce the pop-up menu.

Click here to add special effects to the object's fill.

# AutoShapes

AutoShapes are a new Word 97 feature which allow you automatically to insert commonly used shapes, many of which otherwise might take you some time to draw. To insert an AutoShape, do the following:

*If you plan to use several AutoShapes in one session, you can simply drag one of the submenu palettes away from the main menu, to create a floating palette. It will then stay on-screen when the AutoShapes menu disappears.*

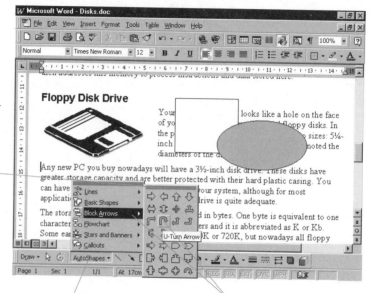

| **Click on the AutoShapes button.**

2 **Select an AutoShapes category, then click on a specific shape.**

3 Click in the area of your document where you want the AutoShape to appear.

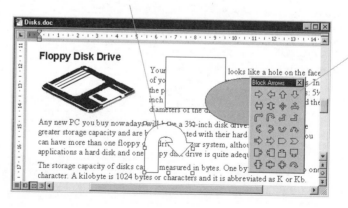

Floating palette (see Hot Tip).

# Formatting Shapes

Many of the properties of objects can be amended by accessing the pop-up menus provided by the Drawing toolbar. However, by right-clicking on a shape, you can summon a dialog box that allows you to change many of the shape's properties in one fell swoop. Right-click on the AutoShape whose format you want to change, choose "Format AutoShape" from the pop-up menu, then select the appropriate tab...

*To set the properties for more than one shape, you should first select all the shapes you want to change. To do this, you have two options:*

*1) Click successively on each object while holding down the Shift button; or*

*2) Click in the document area and drag a selection box around all of the objects.*

*Once all the objects are selected, change the properties as you would for a single object (e.g., right-click on any object, then select "Format AutoShape" from the pop-up menu).*

## The Colors and Lines Tab

Use this to set the shape's fill and line attributes.

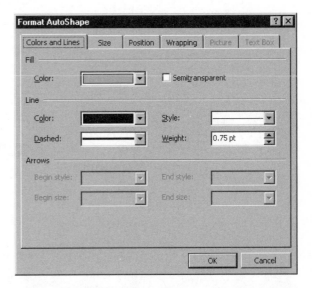

## The Size Tab

Use this to set the shape's dimensions, scale properties and rotation value.

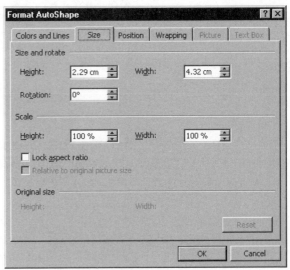

## The Position Tab

From here you can set the coordinates used to determine the object's precise position on the page.

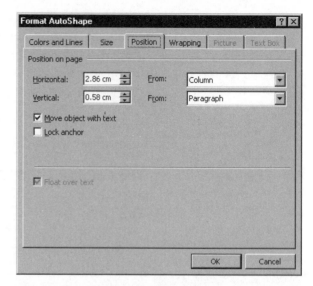

## The Wrapping Tab

Here you can control the way text wraps around the AutoShape.

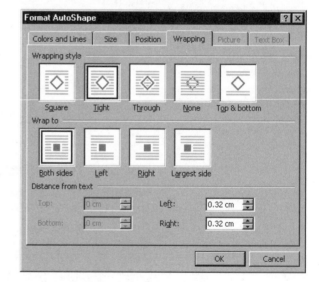

## Setting AutoShape Defaults

To set the properties that all AutoShapes will have when they are created, do the following:

1. Format an existing AutoShape using the Drawing toolbar or the Format AutoShape dialog.

2. Right-click on the shape, then select Set AutoShape Defaults.

# Changing Object Order

When you place a new image or shape in a document, it appears in front of all the other objects that were inserted before it. To change the relative order of objects subsequently, select the object(s) to move, then...

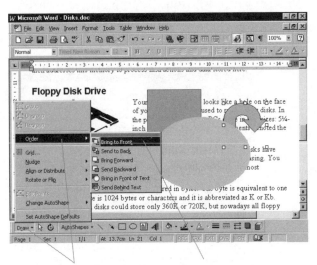

| 1 Click on the Draw menu button and rest the cursor over the Order heading. | 2 Select whether to send the object in front of or behind all other objects, or whether to send it back or forward just one step. |

## Sending Objects Behind the Text Layer

By default, all graphic objects appear in front of the text in your document. However, you can send objects behind the text, by selecting "Bring in Front of Text" or "Send Behind Text" from the menu shown above.

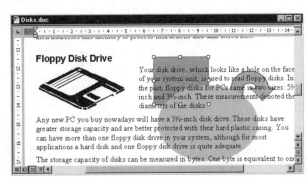

# Grouping and Ungrouping

Once you have placed several objects in your Word document, you may no longer need to treat them separately, but might benefit from treating them as a single object which can be moved and modified easily. To make this possible, you should group the objects, as follows:

Select all of the objects that you want to be grouped together.

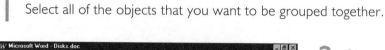
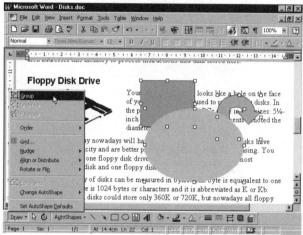

2 Choose Group from the pop-up Draw menu in the Drawing toolbar.

Subsequently, any changes made to the group are applied to all of the grouped objects:

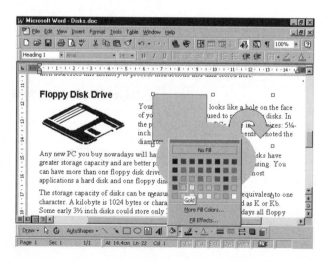

# WordArt

WordArt is a tool you can use to apply a wide range of special graphical effects to type that you use in your Word documents. The objects created by WordArt are treated not as plain text, but as drawing objects, so they can be manipulated further with the tools from the Drawing toolbar that were discussed earlier. To use WordArt, do the following:

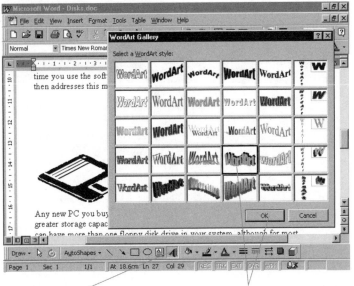

**1** Click on the WordArt button in the Drawing toolbar.

**2** Select a style (you can change it later), then click OK.

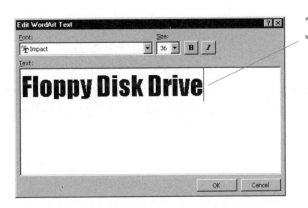

**3** Enter your text here, then click OK.

The WordArt is placed, and can now be edited:

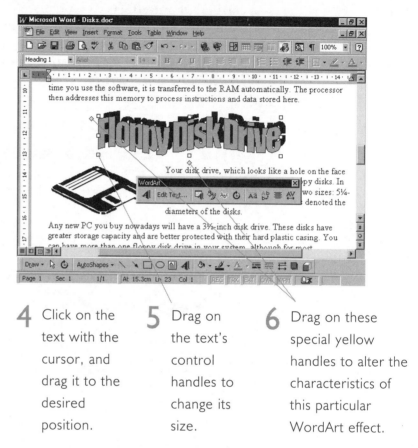

**4** Click on the text with the cursor, and drag it to the desired position.

**5** Drag on the text's control handles to change its size.

**6** Drag on these special yellow handles to alter the characteristics of this particular WordArt effect.

The floating WordArt toolbar appears whenever you select a WordArt object. You can use it for the following functions:

Return to the text-editing box encountered in step 3

Open the Format dialog to alter colour, size, position, text wrap

Allow text to be rotated freely

Toggle between horizontal and vertical text

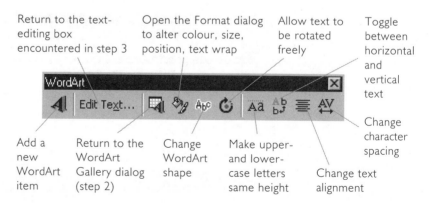

Add a new WordArt item

Return to the WordArt Gallery dialog (step 2)

Change WordArt shape

Make upper- and lower-case letters same height

Change character spacing

Change text alignment

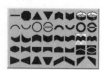

# Tables and Charts

Tables allow you to organise and manage text in rows and columns. If a table contains numeric information, it is possible to depict this in chart form.

## Covers

Chapter Eleven

# Inserting a Table

If you want to insert a simple table of no more than five columns and four rows, it's easiest to use the Table icon in the Standard toolbar:

1 Place the insertion point on a blank line in the document.

2 Click on the Table icon in the Standard toolbar, and in the pop-up table box, drag downwards and to the right.

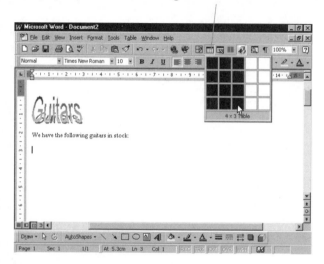

The further you drag, the larger the table. In this case a table of 4 rows and 3 columns is being created.

The table is inserted into your document:

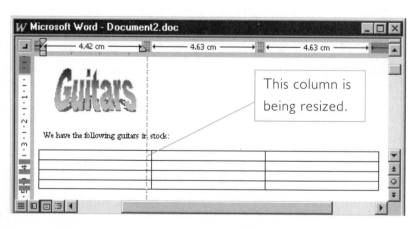

This column is being resized.

# Drawing a Table

Word 97 has a brand new feature that allows you to draw a table directly into your document, without using dialogs or pop-up boxes.

There is an alternative way to begin drawing a table and specify the width of its columns visually: in normal text-entry mode, enter a line using plus and minus symbols, like this...
+---+------+------+
When you press Return, Word will automatically convert this into the first line of a table, the plus signs becoming column boundaries. If this doesn't work, select Tools> AutoCorrect, choose the "AutoFormat As You Type" tab, and check the "Tables" box.

| Select "Draw Table" from the Table menu. The Tables and Borders toolbar appears:

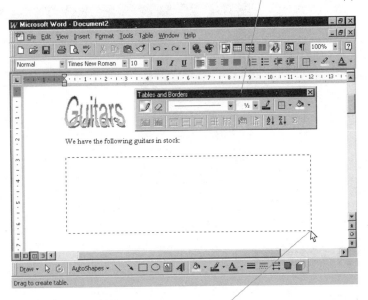

2 Drag an initial shape for the table within your document.

3 Click and drag anywhere in your table to draw a column or row boundary.

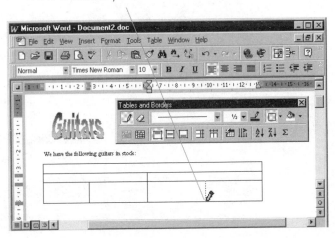

# Entering Text

You can add text to your table by clicking in each cell in turn. All the normal formatting commands still apply.

A quick way to get to the next cell is to press Tab. Shift+ Tab takes you back to the previous cell.

*If you actually need to enter a Tab character, press Control+Tab.*

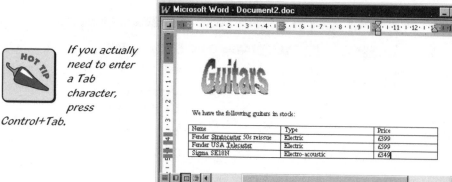

You can have more than one line within each cell. The Table row will expand to accommodate any extra text.

# Formatting

*The same applies to columns. To select, click slightly above the top cell of the column.*

You can format the contents of a whole row or column – or several rows or columns – at once. To select a row, drag across it, or click in the space just to its left.

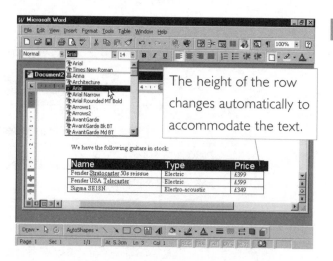

The height of the row changes automatically to accommodate the text.

Make your changes to the selected cells using the normal text-editing features.

# Inserting a Row/Column

*When inserting a row, you should select the row below the point where you want the new one to be inserted.*

To insert a column into an existing table, do the following:

**1** Select the column to the right of where you'd like the new cells.

**2** Click the right mouse button on the selected column, and choose "Insert Columns" from the pop-up menu.

*To insert more than one row or column, select the amount of rows or columns you want inserted before right-clicking.*

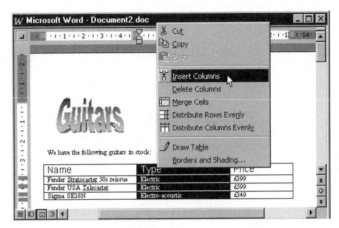

A new column is inserted to the left of the selected one.

# Cutting and Pasting

**1** Select the row/column or cells.

**2** Right-click on the selected cells and choose "Cut" from the pop-up menu.

**3** Select the destination row/column or cells.

**4** Right click on the selected cells and choose "Paste…" from the pop-up menu.

The text is pasted back into the table, immediately above the selected row, or to the left of the selected column.

# Controlling Height and Width

1 Select the cell(s) to change.

2 Choose "Cell Height and Width" from the Table menu.

3 Click on the Row tab, then the Column tab to see all the options available.

"Auto" sizes rows/columns according to the text inside.

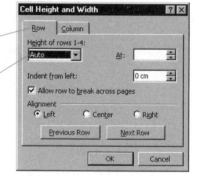

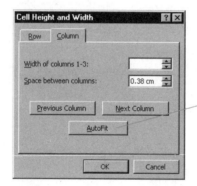

The AutoFit button proportions the column widths on the basis of the table size and the contents of the columns.

# Merging Cells

Any number of adjacent cells can be merged to create a single cell, by selecting the cells and then choosing "Merge Cells" from the Table menu.

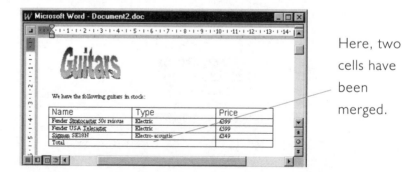

Here, two cells have been merged.

# Formulae

If you want one cell of a table to display a number derived from a calculation based on the numeric contents of other cells, Word can insert a code to perform this task automatically. In this example, we want to total the price of the three guitars in the table.

1 Click in the cell which is the destination for the calculation.

2 Choose "Formula" from the Table menu.

*For the Sum function to work properly, all rows above the current cell must have the same number of columns. If you merged the cells for the last example, you will need to split them again (choose "Split Cells" from the Table menu).*

3 Enter the formula or select from the list of "Paste functions". Word correctly suggests the "=SUM(ABOVE)" function, which adds up the contents of the cells above the destination cell.

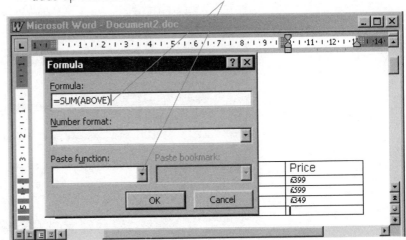

*Unlike a spreadsheet (such as Excel), Word does not automatically update the contents of cells containing formulas when the values of cells used in the equation are changed. To update a formula, right-click on the cell and choose "Update Field" from the pop-up menu.*

4 Click OK. The total is displayed in the destination cell:

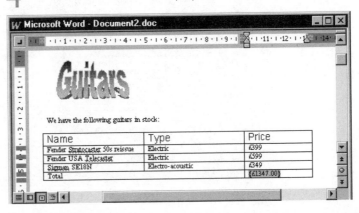

# Borders and Shading

Word 97 allows you to enhance your tables very easily using the Borders and Shading dialog. To use it, do the following:

1. Select either the entire table or just a range of cells.

2. Right-click on the selected cells and choose "Borders and Shading" from the pop-up menu.

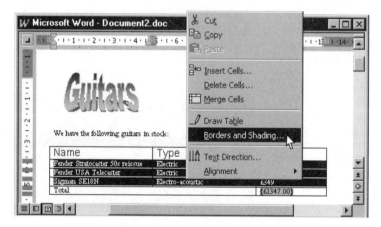

3. If necessary, activate the Borders tab and choose your borders options.

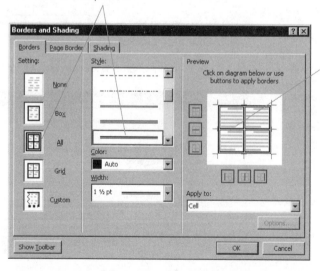

You can click on various parts of this diagram to activate different perimeter and internal lines.

4 Now click on the Shading tab and set your shading
preferences.

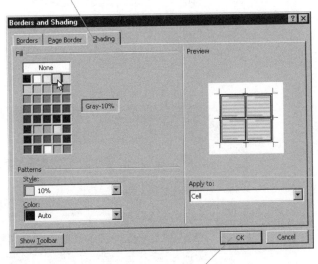

5 Click "OK". Your selected cells now have a border and
shading applied:

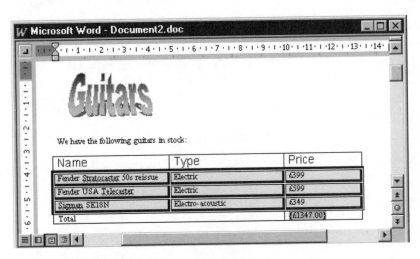

In the example above, the Borders and Shading dialog box
has been used to alter the style of all the lines in the selected
area, and to give those cells a fill of 10% grey.

# Table AutoFormat

As an alternative to defining a table's format piece by piece (i.e., specifying the font, borders, shading, etc.), Word 97 allows you to apply many different pre-defined formats to existing tables. To use AutoFormat, do the following:

**1** Select the table.

**2** Choose "Table AutoFormat" from the Table menu, or click on this button.

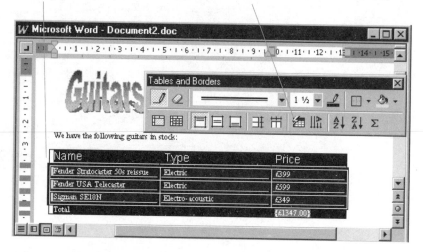

The following dialog appears:

**3** Choose a Format style.

The AutoFormat preview reflects the changes you are about to make.

**4** Select which elements of the table you want the AutoFormat to apply to.

**5** Click OK to apply your changes.

The changes that you have just specified are applied automatically to your table:

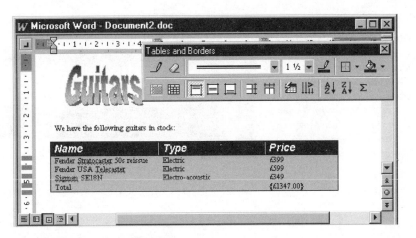

# Using the Tables and Borders Toolbar

You can use the Tables and Borders toolbar to make many of the formatting changes that we have discussed earlier in this chapter. If it is not already activated, select View>Toolbars>Tables and Borders, or click on the appropriate icon in the Standard toolbar:

The Tables and Borders toolbar offers the following functions:

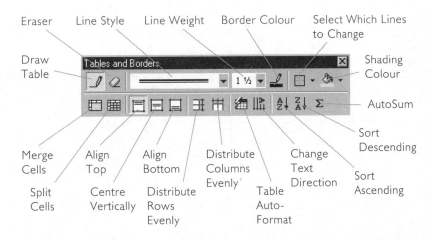

# Creating a Chart from a Table

You can use the Microsoft Graph 97 application to convert a table you have created into an attractive chart.

1 Select the data in the table.

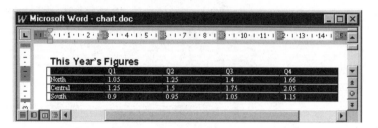

2 Choose "Object" from the Insert Menu.

3 Choose "Microsoft Graph 97 Chart" from the "Create New" tab of the Object dialog, then click OK.

Microsoft Graph 97 automatically generates a suitable graph based on your data, and places it in your document:

*You can also activate the Chart application by clicking on the Chart tool: If this is not visible in Word 97, then right-click on a toolbar and choose "Customise". The Chart icon is available under the "Insert" category. From here you can drag it onto any toolbar.*

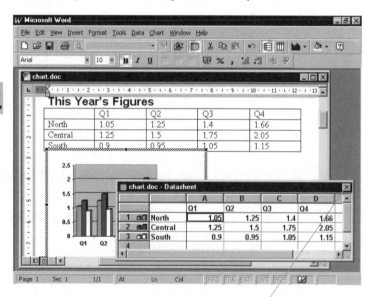

4 If you don't want to amend your data yet, close this window.

# Formatting a Chart

Once your chart is placed in your document, you can very easily edit it, to amend the format that Microsoft Graph applied by default.

I Double-click on the chart to open it for editing; this striped border appears around it, and Special Microsoft Graph icons appear in the toolbar.

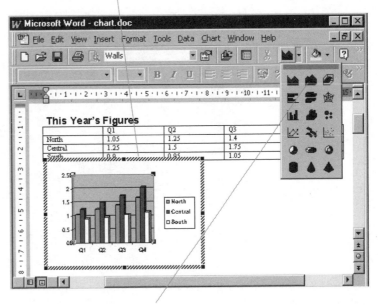

*Microsoft Graph 97 uses two main windows, one for the data and one for the chart itself. You can turn the Datasheet on and off using the View menu, or the Datasheet icon on the toolbar:*

2 To change the type of chart, click on the arrow to the right of the Chart type icon and select an option from the palette.

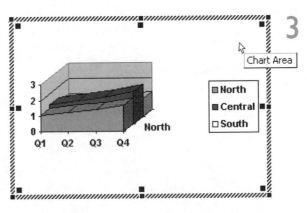

3 To change the properties of a 3D graph, rest your cursor over the chart area until the "Chart Area" bubble appears, then right-click.

**4** In the pop-up menu that appears, select "3-D View".

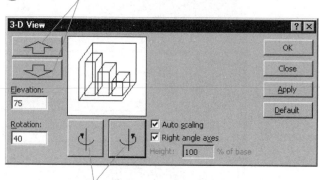

Clicking here would produce a dialog that offers an alternative way of selecting the chart type from the method in step 2.

**5** Click here to change the elevation of the view.

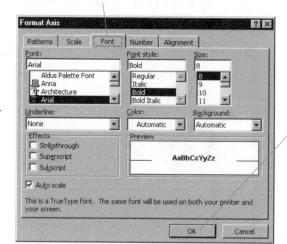

**6** Click here to change the degree of rotation.

**7** To change the properties of an individual chart element, double-click on it. Here, the font properties of the axis legends are being changed.

*When changing the format of a chart, always use the bubbles that appear when you rest your cursor over a chart area. You can then be sure that you are about to format the area that you mean to, before you double-click or right-click on it.*

**8** Click OK to apply your changes.

# Importing Data into a Table

To import data from an external source into a table, make sure the table is open for editing (it will have a striped border around it, and the Microsoft Graph toolbar will appear), then do the following:

| Select "Import File" from the Edit menu.

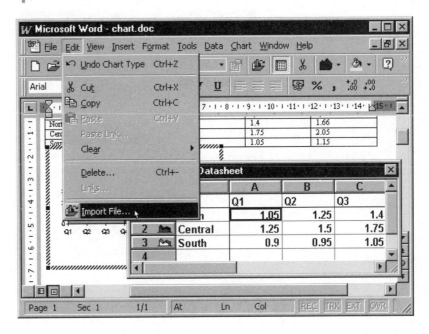

2 In the Import File dialog, select the file you want to import, then click Open. Here, data from a Microsoft Excel spreadsheet is being imported. This data will then be incorporated into the chart.

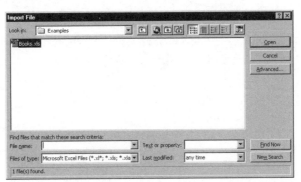

# Chart Number Format

You can change the number format of any of the data used to create your chart. Do the following:

1 Select some or all the cells in the Datasheet window.

2 Choose "Number" from the Format menu.

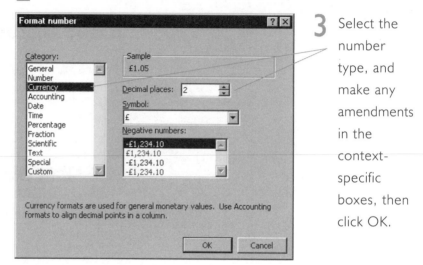

3 Select the number type, and make any amendments in the context-specific boxes, then click OK.

# Returning to Word

When you are working on a chart, you are effectively not using Word, but the Microsoft Graph application. This means that the menu options and toolbar icons that you see are relevant only to Microsoft Graph. To exit this mode and return to the normal Word 97 screen, simply click your cursor anywhere outside the chart area; the Word toolbars and menu options will then return.

# On-line and Internet Documents

Word 97 features many brand-new innovations relating to the Internet and documents intended for viewing on-line or on the World-Wide Web. Features normally used by web pages, such as hyperlinks, can also be incorporated in standard Word documents, allowing instant access of files stored locally or anywhere on the Internet. Word 97 allows automatic editing of HTML web pages, using an intuitive drag-and-drop interface; the Web Page Wizard even sets up the basic outline of your pages for you.

## Covers

Chapter Twelve

# Introduction

In the past, word-processors were used as tools for producing letters, reports, etc., and little else. Recent years have seen popular word-processors become embellished with new graphically-oriented features, which previously would have been found only in top-end Desktop Publishing packages – but until recently, the aim of most people using a word-processor was to produce something that would ultimately be output on paper. However, the growing importance of the Internet, and of Intranet environments, has seen a change in this situation: communication of the sort which was once conducted on paper is now being carried out in a purely electronic medium.

This electronic communication is carried out in a variety of forms, depending on what is being said. The World-Wide Web resembles a huge magazine containing millions of linked pages, with text and pictures on any topic imaginable, and is a type of broadcasting; while e-mail, in its simplest form, is restricted to text, and is essentially a means of one person communicating with one other person.

However, these boundaries are beginning to be blurred. Word, for example, allows you to create an electronic document which is not simply a string of text (as an e-mail is), but which may contain animated text, pictures, sounds, videos, and links to other similar documents or web pages anywhere on the Internet. In fact, any document which you create in Word 97 (or in any element of Office 97) may be placed on the Internet. Alternatively, if you want to send a simple e-mail, you can use WordMail, a feature of Word with several e-mail-oriented facilities, to prepare your message.

Word also allows you to create web pages in the web's native format, HTML (HyperText Mark-up Language), without having to learn the many HTML codes. You can either use the Web Page Wizard to create a new HTML document quickly and easily, from scratch, or you can convert an existing Word document.

# Using the Web Page Wizard

The Web Page Wizard is the most effective way of using Word to create an HTML document, and allows you more control over the finished product than you would have if you converted an existing Word document. To launch it, do the following:

1 Select New... from the File menu.

2 Select the Web Pages tab.

3 Double-click here.

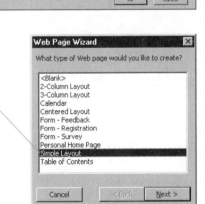

4 Select a layout type from this list, then click Next.

As you click on different layout titles, their appearance will be reflected in the new document window that Word has created.

5 Click a visual style from the dialog box that follows, then click Finish. The new web page will be displayed.

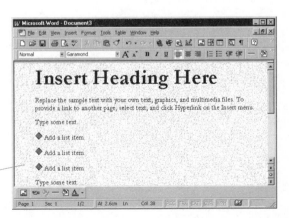

**6** Begin to replace the filler text with your own message

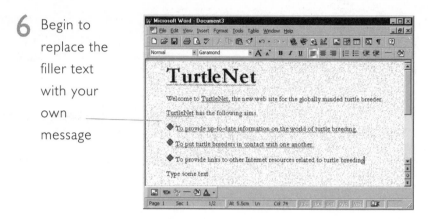

**7** To insert an image into your HTML document, right-click at the place where you want the picture to be inserted, then select "Picture" from the pop-up menu.

**8** Select an image file, then click "Insert".

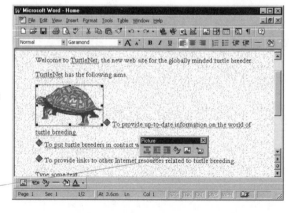

**9** The image is inserted. To fine-tune the layout, drag the image with your cursor, and use these buttons to control the text wrap.

"Right Wrapping" has been selected for this image: the text flows to its right.

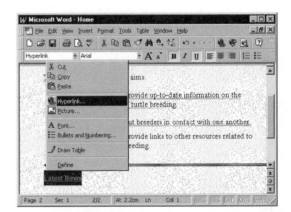

**10** These blue text items are dummy *hyperlinks* to other Web pages. You could modify them, but it's easiest to start from scratch. Erase them, then type in some text…

**11** Select the text, then right-click on it. Choose "Hyperlink" from the pop-up menu.

*From your home page you can provide hyperlinks to local pages (i.e., HTML files located in the same folder as the home page) or Web pages located anywhere on the Internet. You can use the Browse button in the Internet Hyperlink dialog to locate the path for any local or (if you are on-line) Internet page.*

**12** Enter the address of the document you want to link to, then click OK. The hyperlink text you selected will now be highlighted in blue.

# Adding Sound and Video

Most web pages are a collection of text, images and links to other pages. However, as the multimedia capabilities of PCs increase, other types of media are becoming ever more common on the web. For example, you can place video clips on your web pages, and add some background music that will play as people view your page. Doing this is very simple using Word 97's HTML-handling facilities.

### Inserting a Video

1 Place the cursor where you want to insert your video.

2 Select "Video" from the Insert menu.

3 Enter the file name of the video you want to insert.

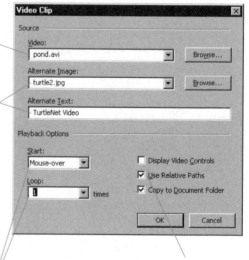

4 (Optional) Enter the file name of an image and/or a text description that will be seen by people whose web browsers cannot handle video files.

5 Specify when the video will play, and how many times. Here, it is set to play when the cursor is passed over it.

6 Make sure this box is checked if you want to use relative path names: i.e., if you want the files you name to be sought in a folder relative to the one that the HTML document is in.

7 Click OK to place the video...

8 Alter the size of the video with the control handles.

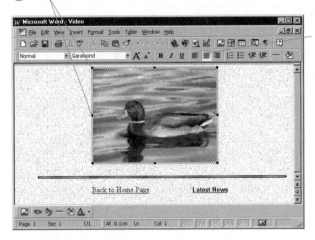

9 Use the alignment buttons just as you would with a still image or a piece of text.

## Adding Background Music

You can add background music to your web page just as easily as adding a video. This music can be a *.wav sound file, a MIDI file, or any of several other formats. Whenever someone accesses your page, this music is played, as long as their web browser allows background music to be played, and only if they have a suitable driver for that sort of sound file.

1 With the your HTML file open, select Insert>Background Sound>Properties.

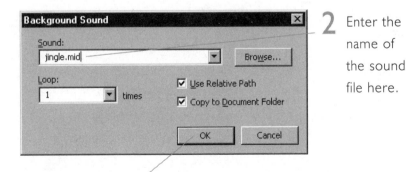

2 Enter the name of the sound file here.

3 Click OK to insert the background music file.

# Hyperlinks

*If Word doesn't convert link addresses like this to hyperlinks by underlining them and changing their colour, you may need to change your AutoFormat settings. Choose AutoCorrect from the Tools menu, then select the "AutoFormat As You Type" tab. Make sure the "Replace... Internet and network paths with hyperlinks" option is checked.*

In the earlier topic "Using the Web Page Wizard", hyperlinks were used to provide a method of moving between one HTML document and another. In Word 97, you are not restricted to using hyperlinks in HTML pages: you can place them in any normal Word document, to link to another place in the same document, to another Word document on your hard drive or a local network, or to a file anywhere on the Internet or an Intranet.

## AutoFormatting Hyperlinks As You Type

By default, Word 97's AutoFormat feature will automatically convert any piece of text that looks like an Internet address or other file location to a hyperlink. These addresses must be in the standard URL format, with which you will be familiar if you have any experience of using a web browser:

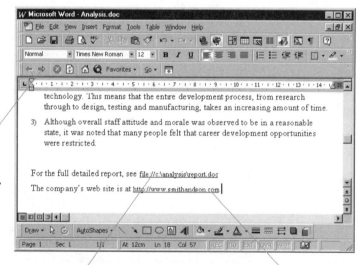

*Click on these arrows to move backwards and forwards through documents and web pages you have visited recently.*

This is a link to a Word file on the same hard drive as the current document. Note the prefix "file://" – if this weren't used, Word wouldn't recognise it as a file location.

This is an Internet URL, linking to a web site. You must be connected to the Internet for this to work.

## Inserting Hyperlinks Manually

The AutoFormat method is fine for converting actual Internet addresses and file locations to hyperlinks, but most hyperlink markers do not take this format; rather, the hyperlink is represented by some more meaningful text, or an image. You can use Word to create either sort of hyperlink, as follows:

1 Select the text or image that the user will click on to jump to your linked file or web site.

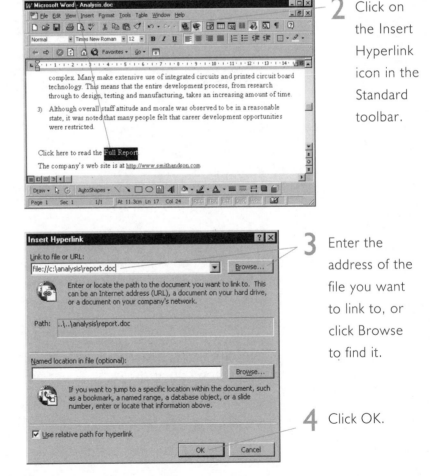

2 Click on the Insert Hyperlink icon in the Standard toolbar.

3 Enter the address of the file you want to link to, or click Browse to find it.

4 Click OK.

The text that you highlighted will now be marked as a link.

# Using WordMail

*If Word is not currently set as your e-mail editor, do the following:*

- *In Outlook, choose Tools>Options, select the E-mail tab, then check the "Use Microsoft Word as the e-mail editor" checkbox; or...*

- *In Exchange, choose Compose>WordMail Options, then check the "Enable Word as e-mail editor" checkbox.*

## Using Word as Your E-mail Editor

If you use Microsoft Outlook or Exchange, and you have set Word as your e-mail editor (see the tip), your e-mail composition can be enhanced by many Word 97 features, such as spelling and grammar checking, version tracking and the use of tables.

Here, Outlook has summoned Word to compose an e-mail message; Word has highlighted a spelling mistake.

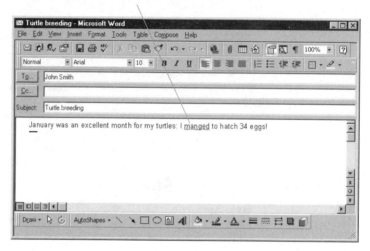

## Enclosing Word Documents in E-mail Messages

If you have created a Word document which you want to send someone via e-mail, you can enclose it in an e-mail message. With the document active, do the following:

1 Select File>Send to>Mail Recipient.

Outlook or Exchange will be launched, with a Word document icon at the top of a new e-mail message area.

2 In the message body, add an introduction to the Word document if you want.

3 Enter a subject line and the recipient's e-mail address, then click the Send to Mail Recipient icon. ✉

# The Reviewing Toolbar

*Animated text is another feature you can use in on-line documents: refer to the topic "The Font Dialog Box" in Chapter 3.*

Word 97 incorporates several sophisticated features that allow you to review documents clearly, and track the various stages of these reviews. The Reviewing toolbar contains icons that allow you to access these features easily. To display it, select Toolbars>Reviewing from the View menu:

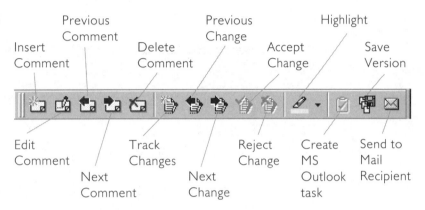

Insert Comment

Previous Comment

Delete Comment

Previous Change

Accept Change

Highlight

Save Version

Edit Comment

Next Comment

Track Changes

Next Change

Reject Change

Create MS Outlook task

Send to Mail Recipient

# Inserting Comments

To insert a comment on a section of your document, do the following:

1. Highlight the text on which you wish to comment.

2. Click the Insert Comment icon.

3. Enter your remarks in the comments box that appears.

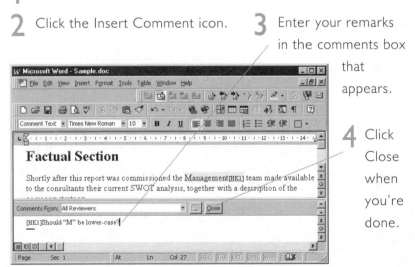

4. Click Close when you're done.

# Highlighting Text

If you want to mark a piece of text without appending any additional notes, you can highlight it, just as if you were using a real highlighter pen on paper. To do this, follow either of the steps below:

1 Select your text with the cursor tool, then click on the Highlighter icon.

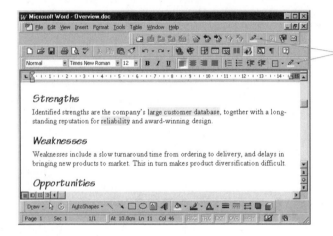

There are Highlighter icons in both the Reviewing toolbar and the Formatting toolbar.

2 Click on the Highlighter icon first, to enter Highlighter mode, then highlight as many different pieces of text as you want. To return to normal text-editing mode, click on the Highlighter icon again.

You are not restricted to using a single colour for the highlighter; this allows you to use different colours for different topics. Do the following:

Click on the arrow to the right of the Highlighter icon, then choose a new colour from the drop-down menu. To remove highlighting, click on "None".

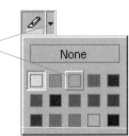

# Versioning

Another new Word 97 feature which can be accessed from the Reviewing toolbar is the facility to save the various stages of the evolution of a document, allowing you to see how its content has developed, and (if appropriate) which of the different authors of a document have made which changes. To save a new version of a document, do the following:

**1** Click on the Save Version icon in the Reviewing toolbar.

The following dialog box appears:

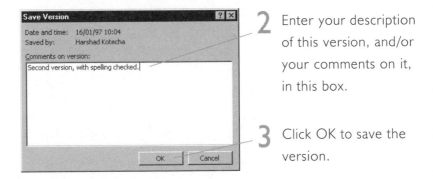

**2** Enter your description of this version, and/or your comments on it, in this box.

**3** Click OK to save the version.

To review the different versions of a document, follow these steps:

**1** Select "Versions" from the File menu.

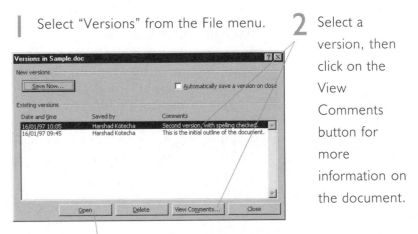

**2** Select a version, then click on the View Comments button for more information on the document.

**3** Click here to open the selected version of the document.

# Collaborating on Documents

If each of the different reviewers of a document works from a different computer, which is used by them alone, then there should be no need to alter the reviewer information, as this should have been established when Word 97 was installed. However, if a computer is shared by a number of people to review Word documents, then the user information should be changed whenever a reviewer begins, so that it is clear who made which comments.

1 Select "Options" from the Tools menu.

2 Choose the User Information tab.

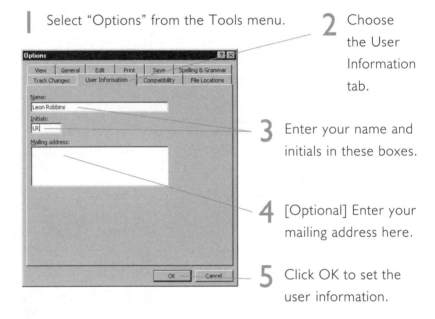

3 Enter your name and initials in these boxes.

4 [Optional] Enter your mailing address here.

5 Click OK to set the user information.

## Merging Documents

If a number of reviewers have been working together on the same document by updating the same Word file, then the sum of all their efforts is collected in the most up-to-date version of the document. However, if different reviewers have made changes to a document and saved the results as a different file (e.g., to take the document away to work on at home), it is possible to merge the files back into one document

1 With one of the files open, select Tools>Merge Documents.

2 In the file dialog that appears, double-click on the file to merge.

# Index

# O

# P

# R

# S